VICTORY AFTER DIVORCE
Start Your Successful Life NOW

Kim Edmiston

10-10-10
Publishing

Publisher
10-10-10 Publishing
Markham, ON   Canada

Printed in Canada and the United States of America

*To every reader of this book who is facing
the emotional struggles of divorce,
and the excitement of success, you got this!
May my experience give you the extra support
and guidance to achieve your dreams.*

*To my kids, Alex and Brayden with all my love,
you gave me the strength when I didn't think I could go on.
I hope this teaches you that you can achieve anything
if you put your mind to it.*

Table of Contents

Acknowledgements

Raymond Aaron, who taught me so much, and still every day three very important words, "don't add time" run around in my head and I get the job done, faster and more efficiently. Although this is still a work in progress, I am doing better.

To the amazing **Loral Langemeier,** who started me on this journey of writing a book through an event I attended. I connected with her journey as a single mom; it's up to me, and only me.

Shelagh Cummins, my personal business coach for many years. I never knew a business coach was important to the success of a business until I met Shelagh. Shelagh, you have supported me every step of the way, before, during and after divorce. You helped me grow every day. You lit the fire under me when I needed it, and you helped me find the right road to success. You stand out from the crowd because you taught me that it wasn't just about my business growing and being healthy; it was about me too.

To my **dad**, my mentor in heaven, thank you for your support, love and encouragement along the way. You are always my hero. You once said to me, "The finance industry treated me well and gave a good living; I hope it will do the same for you." Following in your footsteps with your words of encouragement and praise has kept me moving forward.

To my brother **David** in heaven, thank you for encouraging me to write this book and supporting me along the way until you joined Dad. Your courage and strength allowed me to finish my book, and I can still hear your laughter when we spoke about my book.

My **mom**, my friend, my biggest fan. The support and love that you've given me throughout my life is never forgotten and always appreciated. We went from the three musketeers to the dynamic duo, and although Dad is missed daily we still manage to have some laughs and tears when the cardinals fly.

To my sister **Linda,** brother-in-law **Joe** and sister-in-Law **Melanie**, thank you for supporting my crazy life with every path I've taken with love and smiles and a few glasses of wine along the way.

Family is number one through everything; **Kristen** and **Amanda Barnes**, **Caitlin and Brian Brennan**, my nieces and nephew, I've watched you all grow into amazing, successful, caring adults. I couldn't be prouder of you. Much love to all of you.

The one and only that is always by my side to support me, praise me, laugh with me and cry with me. **Shannon Reddom**, we got this!

Jamie Smith and Yvonne Yu, when I bought my home three years after the separation I was excited that I was on the right track. When I met you, I felt blessed to have such amazing neighbours. From baking and food sampling from Yvonne, to snow plowing and small repairs from Jamie. But it was not just what you did, it was the driveway conversations, the backyard giggles and the amazing friends you have become, not just to me but to my kids too.

John Hill, I may not share in your love of cars or know what you're speaking about, but I do enjoy a summer ride with the top down watching the sun set. Over the years our friendship has grown, and the support, love and laughs you've brought to my life mean so much to me.

Dave Barry, our friendship has lasted the test of time, from our days of high school through the years, and you are still by my side. Although we lost touch for a while you've been there for me since we reconnected, with your thoughtfulness always. Forever you will always be my big brother who's always been by my side with laughs, love and support.

James Calabro, you took a chance on me and the kids, allowing us to put a roof over our heads. You acted on your heart; you believed me when I said I'd never let you down. Having a home was our first step to moving on and the first step of my journey.

Georgina Cares Fund, for allowing my daughter to continue her horseback riding in the first year of my separation when I just couldn't afford it. Keeping her going to support her emotionally with her one true love made such a difference.

Lakeside Public School, with special thanks to Ms Kocot, for giving me and my kids a special Christmas in 2016 when I couldn't. You stepped in without me even knowing, and your thoughtfulness has never been forgotten over the years. It is still my favourite Christmas as you turned tough times into the best of times with your kindness.

Gineen and Jennifer, for the many years of cheers, tears and beers, we were always there for each other.

Sam Farhat and Rob Schuyler, you've become great friends over the years, and whenever I am stuck with my house repairs you're always there to assist me. The many laughs we've shared, especially in the early days, helped me to find my smile again. You've become part of my family.

Rogers TV Georgina - Jim and Jennifer Anderson, Lynda Q, Patty Parsons, Jeremiah. Thank you for always supporting and promoting our community and the people.

Lynda and Ralph Quirino, when I started on my new journey as a single mom I was so lucky to have such amazing neighbours who were always there to help me, support me and make me laugh. A friendship that has continued even after I moved.

Helen and Darlene, what started as a business meeting has become many years of friendship and good laughs, with many more to come.

Craig Wallace, you have kept me laughing over the years you seem to know when I need a quick hello or a giggle.

To my **social media friends**, including my many high school friends from many years ago, thank you for always supporting me along my journey with words of wisdom, support and love.

Chris, my ex-husband, we walked down a very difficult path but along the way we started to work together. We proved that we can live our separate lives but still help each other and be there together to help, support and love our children.

My dog **Peter,** you changed my life for the better, and you made every day worthwhile, even the tough ones. You truly are my best friend and I will be there for you forever. My gift to you recently was a new friend, **Baxter,** who I know has brought you hours of fun playtime while I am working.

Testimonials

I have known, worked, and interacted with Kim for many years now. This woman is a tour de force. I worked with Kim when we were both community producers at a local TV station, and she was organized and disciplined and knew her stuff. I watched her run her business, Momstown, with such ease and panache. I witnessed her marriage fall apart as she was very candid with her friends about her experience. Most importantly, I witnessed an even greater loss than her marriage – and that was the loss of her father.

These were back-to-back events that would break the best of us. Maybe it did break her, but that is where the greatest lesson of life occur. Kim meets those lessons head on. Through will, determination, courage and being a single parent, Kim did not give in and did not give up, but instead faced her circumstances and started working towards a new future, and a new life. Kim started new and proved that there is life after divorce. Well done and congratulations my friend!

Patty Parsons
TV Host / Producer

I would say that I've known Kim for a lifetime. She has helped me tackle all the rough times in life, and we have laughed and shared the good times. She has supported me throughout my journey; she is a wonderful woman and a true friend.

Shannon Reddom

Foreword

Have you recently gone through a divorce? Are you searching for a way to move past the difficult times, and truly heal? Are you trying to find answers, but are unsure where to turn?

At times It can be difficult to heal the repercussions of divorce; however, that feeling is only temporary. You can create a new and better future for yourself; and with determination, you can create success all on your own. Believe in yourself!

Kim Edmiston wrote *Victory After Divorce* so she could share with you her personal journey through divorce, to starting her own business. It is important that you take time to grieve the dreams you've lost; however, it is important to look toward the future, and focus on the positive changes you can make.

This book will show you that you can become successful even when darkness falls on you. Kim created an entirely new life for herself because she believed she could do so. She wanted to be financially free, so she made things happen for herself. And you can too!

This is an empowering book that will help you to see that you no longer need to dwell on the past, or the difficult times in your life. You can create any life you want, as long as you put in the work and keep believing that you can make it through any hardship.

Be prepared to change your life and get on a better path by reading *Victory After Divorce*. It is a must read if you are looking to overcome your past, begin to heal, and create success within your own life.

Loral Langemeier
The Millionaire Maker

Chapter 1

Where Do You Begin?

*"The best preparation for tomorrow
is doing your best today."*
– H. Jackson Brown, Jr.

Leaving the Past Behind

April 7, 2015 was the day my life changed. My family and I had the normal routine of spending Easter together. After the celebrations were over, my spouse and I made the announcement to the kids that we were separating, and it was time we were to part ways. It was an emotional ride, and the reasons for this are not important here. All I could see was that we were moving on separately; starting a new life, each of us on our own. Two kids' lives were also about to change, and that was not a decision that was made lightly, but we had opened our eyes and realized, it was time.

My husband packed his bag and headed on his way; the kids had gone to their rooms after saying a tearful goodbye to their dad. The house was too quiet. For the first time in many years, there was no laughter, no voices, no arguing; even the dogs had become quiet.

I looked around the house that was once a home, where we had brought two babies, two dogs, and a bunny; where we spent our first years as a married couple, and celebrated many birthdays and holidays with laughter and tears.

It hit me. I was moving on, but this time, I was doing it alone and I was completely terrified.

For some reason in that moment, I couldn't remember the bad days, I only was looking back at the good ones. It's funny how that works sometimes.

I had closed my digital media company in January of 2015, and was currently unemployed. I had some small side gigs, but there was not a lot of income coming in. To say I was terrified is such a drastic understatement. I was sitting alone thinking of the almost ten years of marriage and a few years of dating that was gone now.

We don't get married thinking one day it will end, but for me that is exactly what had just happened. The emotions were overwhelming: anger, sadness, fear; they all hit me all at once. I wanted to scream, I wondered where I had gone wrong, where he'd gone wrong, but those days had passed and it was time to figure out my next move as a single parent and leave those emotions behind me. I had to find a way to move past all of this.

I had a good cry, a glass of wine, and then decided when I woke up in the morning it was behind me. I allowed myself to grieve, but life as I knew it was over, and a new chapter was about to begin. I had to collect my emotions and be strong. I had to move my focus to building a new life and not dwelling on where I had been.

There were good memories and not so good memories, but that is all they were now, memories of my past. There was no point in being angry or sad; I needed to move on and focus on building an amazing new life. It was time to set some goals, the first steps to moving forward.

Tomorrow was a new day, the sun would shine, and I would move forward one step at a time to reach success.

Taking Care of You

As you roll through the process of divorce and starting a new business, it's important to do something good for yourself. For me, although I didn't know it at the time, this "something good" was getting a dog. I wasn't planning on getting a dog, but I had seen him on the internet one day, and a month later, he was a Canadian citizen and had become my best friend in life. He makes me take a break when I am continuously working and forget about caring for myself. He helped me get through the times of loneliness and feeling defeated.

Me time is different for everyone. Maybe it consists of a glass of wine, or a spa day, but as you are going through one of the most emotional times in your life, it is so incredibly important to take time out for you. Starting a business and dealing with your emotions at the same time can be tough. If you don't take that time, there is a good chance you will fail. Not because you weren't trying or working hard, but because you were working so hard without filling your cup, you were unable to accomplish anything because of your mental state.

No matter what your idea of me time is, find something you enjoy, and something that makes you feel good. It is just as important to be strong mentally as it is to be successful. All things come with hard work, but you cannot make it if you are struggling to care for yourself and love the person you see in the mirror.

Setting Goals and Getting Organized

Before I set goals, I had to know what an actual goal was. The dictionary meaning of goals is "the result or achievement toward which effort is directed."

When I first started out on my own, I was flying by the seat of my pants. My coaches kept telling me that I needed to set goals, and for the first few years, I had goals in my head, but for the most part I didn't achieve them. This left me feeling like I failed. I wondered if I should keep striving to build my business or just pack it in.

An example of a recent goal I had was to meet every deadline and requirement of my client's tasks, prior to them requesting it. I wanted to become proactive and less reactive; a hard task for a single mom entrepreneur.

Through the advice of a coach, I now write down my goals every few months, and I don't tuck them away never to be seen again like I once used to. Instead, I hand-write them in a binder that I keep on my desk. Not only do I write them down, but I write notes on how I can achieve these goals. Sometimes I even put timelines in. I do everything I can to ensure that I succeed.

Setting goals is a great way to get you started on your way. Take it from someone that didn't see the value in this in the beginning because I was too busy. Setting goals, and sticking to them, really does work. At times, it can be hard to hold yourself accountable. That's where an accountability coach / mentor is great, because they keep you focused on the end goal and getting there when you hit a brick wall.

Five years ago, I never thought I could run a business that would provide for me and my family, but I have, and I continue to grow each and every year.

My first goal was making enough money to put food on the table and a roof over our head. I worked out the numbers and that goal sat on my monitor on a sticky note.

Court Days

I hated going to court. A day in court consisted of a breakfast of Pepto and a banana. I had always followed the law, so court in itself made me feel like I had done something wrong. During that time, I was sad and angry, and was still unsure of how to release all of that. When the court dates first started, I had my daily phone calls, and the random visit with my best friend, Shannon, which really did so much for me; more than I truly realized at the time.

Those long days of waiting in the courthouse, sitting in front of the judge, had me shaking in my boots hoping that I wouldn't be asked to speak, and if were asked, hoping I would not throw up all over the desk. I could not have done it without the support of my lawyer. She not only handled everything, but she also supported me emotionally.

When we sat in the small closed room together, we'd even have a few laughs on different topics to ease my anxiety. Over time, I learned that as long as I had Helen by my side at the courthouse, I was ok. While I was dealing with a very painful subject, I had someone on my team, and that meant so much to me.

Choosing the right lawyer to get you through these days is very important. If there are kids involved, there is a good chance that the courts will be involved. Nearing the end, I no longer felt the need to have my trusty companion Pepto there as I had gotten more comfortable with the process, thanks to my lawyer.

On October 31, 2019, I walked out of the courthouse. It was an icy, snowy day, and I travelled home in a hurry to get the kids ready for Halloween. I cried, because I knew it was finally behind me, and my divorce papers were being processed. ***It was over.***

The important lesson I learned during these days was that court is hard for everyone, it brings up many emotions, and you can even lose sight of the end goal. I tried to stay focused as best I could and not let my emotions get in the way. I always went alone; I didn't want anyone there with me as I felt it would be harder for me. I found comfort in the conversation with my lawyer. Some people I know said they couldn't go alone, and they always took someone.

You will find what works best for you and that will be the right decision. You'll get through it one day at a time. I remember people saying to me, "Kim, it will get better and you and your ex-husband will one day work together for the kids." At the time, I thought they were crazy, but that day did come and eventually, life got much better.

Moving Forward and Starting My Business

What's next? How do you move forward? Well, number one is not letting your emotions get in the way of your success. Moving forward is about taking action and starting to plan financially for your new life. Make a plan, and discover what you need to be able to move forward. I needed a home for me and my kids, and I needed a career.

What did I need to do to get there, and most importantly, what was I good at? Working a regular job was not an option for me. I had two small kids, and

I needed a career that was time flexible. Self-employment was what I needed to pursue, and it had to be successful because my kids were depending on me.

Here was my thought process ...

I had been a bookkeeper for over twenty years. Even though I had run other businesses, I always did bookkeeping on the side. My first job as a bookkeeper was around 1995. I worked for an ISP in the city. My first day on the job I had a copy of QuickBooks placed on my desk. My job was to learn it, use it, and be the best bookkeeper I could be. For the next five years or so, that's exactly what I did, along with other tasks, in the role of office manager.

Throughout my five years as a bookkeeper, I still felt the longing to do something else. I eventually decided to take a leap and open up an Equestrian Centre in Uxbridge. I left the Toronto Danforth area and moved to the country. This was my first experience of being self-employed, and I took on two businesses (bookkeeping and boarding horses) with no knowledge or help on how to do so. I took care of horses in the early morning, and once they were outside, I did bookkeeping for a few clients in the barn office. On weekends, I would hold special events and clinics with professionals in the equestrian field. I did this for a while, and then eventually decided it was time for me to go back to the city and just focus on the finance side of my career.

Over the next ten years, I held various positions in the finance field, which even included working in data base management for a company in the financial industry. I learned how to use SQL amongst other various tools. In 2005 I got married and shortly thereafter, I got pregnant with my daughter. I left my job to be a stay-at-home mom. Well, that didn't last long, and before I knew it, started doing bookkeeping for some friends and their businesses.

I then decided it was time to start something new, and opened up a licensed company in the digital media field. I hosted live events local to my community with great sponsors. Social media was fairly new and it was a great career while my children were young, and still, I was doing bookkeeping on the side, and for my own company. I did anything, and everything I could to ensure my family, and myself was in a good place financially, and mentally.

In order to figure out the best option for you in terms of starting a new business, you need to determine what you're good at. When I first opened up my business, it was as a virtual assistant. I did event planning, mailings, website, data entry almost anything that would pay the bills I took on. However, I wasn't doing what I was good at and what I enjoyed.

Throughout my time trying to start up my own business and find success, I felt it was necessary and helpful to seek advice from a business coach who knew what my end results were, and also what it would take to get there. Seeking advice from a professional who can better assist in your own goals can be extremely helpful if you are unsure of the next steps to take.

After many conversations with my business coach, I realized I was doing what was in front of me to make money, and not doing what I was good at. I was/am a good bookkeeper and the success that I have acquired over the years has confirmed I made the right choice. Don't do what you think you might be good at, do what you WILL be good at. Look at your history, analyze it, and figure out what it is your good at and enjoy doing. Now you know what this is, it is time to take action!

First Big Steps

Emotions don't go away overnight. As you build your business, your emotions can be a constant struggle. You will have days when you think you've bitten off more than you can chew, days you feel defeated and don't want to get out of bed, and days you feel you are awesome and you can take on the world! Learning to cope with it all at once, while raising your kids and having the weight of the world on your shoulders, is not an easy task, but one step at a time will get you there. Every step in the right direction can make a world of difference.

When I was first separated, I was angry, sad, and emotional. Then one day I said to myself, "It's his loss." That was a huge step for me. I stopped thinking about the years gone by, and instead started looking at the years ahead of me. Nothing was going to stop me from being successful, and the first step was taken. This in no way means that I still don't have a mix of good days and bad days. Instead, I have just learned how to compartmentalize it all. If I am angry, I put that anger into growing my business. Don't let your emotions allow you to fail.

I used to start my day by writing sticky notes and posting them on my monitor. It is a great habit to get into. Sometimes the message was from a TV show I watched, some days it was more of an inspirational or motivational type note, sometimes personal, or a to-do list, and some days, it was just a happy face. No matter the type of note I decided to write myself for the day, it helped because I knew that I was taking that extra step to take care of myself.

Here are some examples of sticky notes that I found helpful:

- I am strong; I can do this
- Marketing with a positive mind = clients

- Success = Motivation; Motivation = Success
- 2 more clients = hiring staff
- I am a successful, confident, independent woman
- Complete client X today = walk in the forest with the dog tomorrow

These sticky notes may sound silly and, honestly, I thought they were too when I started writing them. However, once you get into the routine of doing this, those silly feelings change, and you actually begin to feel better about yourself and the path you are on. It didn't matter to me if it sounded silly. I realized it made a difference in my day, and that is all that mattered, and still matters.

I am a big believer in writing everything down, even the things you think aren't important. They may become important down the road. If you have any interest in starting a business, writing down your thoughts can greatly help you to stay on track, and stay focused on the goals you have in front of you. Your business model may change many times as you take these initial steps; that is all a part of the process. Once you have figured out what kind of business you want to have, if that is what you have set in your mind, the next step is figuring out how to get there.

The ideas and thoughts that you write down will soon be part of a business plan, and everyone needs a business plan. I assisted many people in writing business plans, and they have come to realize how important they are.

Chapter 2

Starting a Business

"Start by doing what's necessary; then do what's possible; and suddenly you are doing the impossible."
— Francis of Assisi

Hiring a Business Coach

Looking to hire a business coach? Well, let's start by looking at what a business coach is. They are considered entrepreneurs who give encouragement, support and guidance to other business owners. They accompany you on your journey, and give assistance in order to help you become successful in your business ventures.

Business coaches know how to see the big picture, and can help you understand what it takes to make it on your own. They will assist in keeping you accountable to ensure you are keeping up with the goals you have set in place for yourself, which will keep you on the right track. To put it simply, a business coach is there for you every step of the way, to keep you on your toes and get you to a place you want to be businesswise and financially. They help you to see the light through the trees.

I have had different kinds of coaches who have assisted me along the way in my business side of my life, as well as my personal life. I have also had what I call my "main" coach who has been with me from day one. She supports me not only by guiding me through the forest but also by helping me with my emotions. I wouldn't be where I am today, with the confidence and successful business I now have, without my business coach.

You can have a coach in your life for a variety of reasons depending on what you are looking to work on or get assistance with. Coaches can be there to help you with many aspects of your life, and can be a great guide when you are unsure of where to go next.

When searching for a good business coach, you need to find someone you like. The emotional connection to someone that is so close to your life and business is important. Be sure to look into their background too. You need someone who has experience in the field, and can provide good recommendations. Most coaches will allow you a one-time meet and greet, often over the phone or by video chat, so take the time to schedule that appointment. You want someone who has put in the time, and is able to show that their hard work has paid off.

You want to ensure that the coach can give you clear and concise steps on how to make it in the business world. People starting a business often rush into it, and make financial decisions that might not be the best ones to make. A coach can help you understand what is important to focus on, and what you can put on the back burner at first.

Most importantly, when looking for a business coach, you want to find someone that you can look up to. You should look for someone who encourages you and helps you to see the big picture. This is someone who will be able to help you get to where you want to be.

To get the most out of your coach, you need to be committed to changing your old way of doing things. The coach you hire may have a different way of running a business, one that you may not have thought of, and one that gets you further ahead than your competitors.

You never know what the coach has to offer, so it's important to listen to all they have to say and not avoid trying something just because you think your way is better. Be open to listening to your coach's ideas, and try something new. Changing things up may just be that golden ticket you were looking for.

Business coaches can help you in a variety of ways, but to begin with, they really like to focus on goal setting. Goals are the stepping stones to get you to where you want to be. They motivate you by helping you see the big picture.

A coach can also help you see the importance of using your time wisely and being productive. While you may have found a way to delegate your time nicely, a coach may have some tips that can help you take it that step further.

Many times, new business owners try to do as much as they can, as quickly as they can. While that may seem like a good idea to get your business up and running as fast as possible, it also will eventually tire you out, and have you feeling like you are doing too much.

Doing everything yourself also leaves you with no free time, which is something that everyone needs in their life whether they are starting a business or not. A coach will ensure that you fit in some time just for you, so you can get a break and re-energize!

Working with a coach that is right for you will help you learn how to use your time wisely, and focus on tasks with the highest importance. They can teach you how to share the work with your employees (if you have employees), or if you are a one-person business, they can show you how to manage your time to get everything done without feeling exhausted and worn down at the end of the day.

Business coaches are also there to help you with the relationships you make when starting a business. Each day, you need to talk with other business owners, customers, people investing in your business; the list goes on! Having a coach by your side can make it easier on you because they know every side of the business. They understand the importance of having strong business relationships and can help you get where you need to be, in order to be successful.

Coaches are there every step of the way, so ensuring you have the right one is crucial. Take the time to do your research, and find someone who fits best in your life and business because they may be assisting you for a long period of time.

Money, Money, Money

What does money mean to you? In the different phases of our life money has different meanings. One thing is constant, however; we can't live without it. When I first started running my own business, the biggest challenge I had was cash flow. How do you start a business without the money to get it off the ground?

These were very tough days! I can remember when I would feed the kids and what was left over was my dinner. I don't even know if they realize today that I did this. Buying groceries was stressful because I didn't always have the money to pay for them but had to figure out how I would feed the kids. There were days I would sit in my car in tears trying to figure out how I could get out of the mess I was in. I got out of it by working hard and getting the cash flow moving.

The first step was a visit to the bank. I had credit cards but was reluctant to use them until I had cash flow. Waiting for my meeting with the bank manager, I was nervous, but I walked away from that meeting with a line of credit for my business, and a line of credit for me personally. I was on my way, but I had to be careful. If I failed, it wasn't just me who would be affected; it was my kids too.

There are other great options, including grants and loans available for startups. I made the mistake of researching this after I'd been in business for a while, and I didn't qualify. Do your research, and find out what you and your type of business qualifies for. I do this for all my clients on a regular basis now. You never know when a new cash opportunity is out there that could help your business. The key is don't get in over your head.

In order to get your business established and bring in some of that cold hard cash, you need to get your name out there. In most cases you are the face of the business and you need to be recognized. This was a big one for me. I knew I had to build my brand, which was me, in order to be successful. I had an established network, so I started there, making phone calls, sending emails, and putting out promos. I worked endless hours to build a clientele.

I used every potential free advertising opportunity I could, including nominations for awards, TV spots with my hometown TV network, trade shows, volunteering, and social media, to name a few. Think outside the box; do the work to make it happen. We will talk about this more in a later chapter.

Three years after splitting up from my ex-husband, and three years after starting my business, I put a down payment on a house. Keep looking at the end victory for yourself, as you keep pushing forward with lots of blood, sweat and tears. You'll get there. There will be days when you want to give up, but push forward until you find the money that will help you live your dreams.

Employee vs Entrepreneur

While an entrepreneur has a different name, the only real difference between an entrepreneur and an employee is in regard to mindset. An employee could easily transition to becoming an entrepreneur by changing the way they see themselves, and taking the steps to become business savvy while working on succeeding at their goals.

During an interview, often you are asked what your weaknesses are. Entrepreneurs tend to avoid looking at weaknesses, choosing instead to focus on the positive. They look at improving their skills instead of compensating for their weaknesses. They like to hone in on their skills and show that they can achieve anything. Employees often tend to focus on their weaknesses. To move into an entrepreneur mindset, step away from the negative and veer towards the positive. Focus on those strengths!

When it comes to task delegation, employees tend to want to get as much done as possible. They want to multi-task and try to focus on a million things at once. Entrepreneurs avoid that, as they have seen that it is almost impossible to successfully multi-task.

Multi-tasking is difficult because our brains cannot successfully focus on several things at once. Our brains run a lot faster if we work on one task at a time. Knowing this, entrepreneurs try to mono-task instead of multi-task, so they can ensure that they did the work to their best ability.

Another major difference between an employee and an entrepreneur is that employees tend to get threatened by people in their workplace who do the job better than them, or by people who appear more intelligent. This is a normal way to think if you are surrounded by people who are looking to take over your job. It is hard to move up on the ladder when there is competition surrounding you.

Instead of fearing people smarter than them, entrepreneurs look to hire those people. They see intelligence as an asset, and strive to find people competent enough to do the job, and do it well. It's important to change your mindset when becoming an entrepreneur so you can view people's strengths as a positive instead of a negative.

Entrepreneurs also understand the importance of taking risk. If they never chose to take any risks, then they most likely would not be in the place they are. Becoming successful in your business usually means you have to take some risks to get there. While there is a small chance you may not succeed, you will never know if don't take the risk to begin with.

Employees tend to do the opposite. They do not want to risk losing their own job, so they avoid taking chances on things. Security is the most important aspect of an employee's job, but without any risk, there is no chance of reward. This is why, in order to become an entrepreneur; you need to learn to take some risks.

To move up in the business world may seem like a scary thought, but setting goals and believing in yourself are important steps to take when looking to become an entrepreneur. Don't let fear stop you from making your dreams come true.

How Can My Kids and Family Help Me?

As a single mom, it's often hard to find a balance between working from home, juggling the kids, and getting your work done. I know you've been there, those days you want to pull out your hair because the phone is ringing and it's not clients, it's a family member or friend that just wants to shoot the shit because they're bored or they miss you. Of course, there is the all too famous "Mom, I'm hungry" lament from the kids as well. I struggled for years with this until finally I got tired of playing catch-up with my business on a weekly basis.

My first step is rectifying the situation was to put business hours in place. Now, my family and friends know not to call during office hours unless it's an emergency. Scheduled visits only, no drop-ins that screw up the entire day and make me miss deadlines. Hey, I love my family and friends but I need to make a living too. Working from home makes it difficult for people to understand the importance of a schedule; they often think that because you're always there it doesn't matter when people call or drop in. But truthfully, it does.

I stopped feeling guilty for trying to juggle it all and I finally stepped up and told them how it was. Yes, I work from home but the key word in there is W-O-R-K. I told them, if they wanted to help me be successful, they had to understand and comply with my new office hours and rules. To my surprise, they did. They weren't mad at me, I didn't disappoint anyone, and I started meeting my deadlines without working until 5am.

If my kids are home for a snow day, online school or even a weekend, I no longer answer to "Mom, I'm hungry." One day I turned it around and said, "Kids, I'm hungry." I went back to work, and a few minutes later I found, to my surprise, a smiling child walking into my office with lunch made and delivered with a smile. HA! I figured it out, I had to ask, and I had to speak up. My kids have pitched in from day one, doing the dishes, unpacking the groceries, and even making dinner at times when I am really swamped.

The key to success here was I had to ask; I had to explain my situation. The more I let the kids and family know how busy I was, and that I needed help where they could help, the more I had the time to dedicate to my office uninterrupted. Oh, I still have days when I want to pull my hair out, but after letting everyone know I was struggling due to the interruptions, they stepped up and enabled me to work on a more steady basis and get the job done.

Now that they respect me and my business, I in turn give it back to them as a reward. Not with treats or gifts but with my time. Maybe it was lunch with my mom, or popcorn and movie with my son, or a night at the barn watching my daughter ride. These are the things they wanted. If I am able to get my work done because everyone is pitching in, then I am able to take the time to spend with my loved ones.

At the end of the day, it comes down to communication. If you are communicating with your loved ones about how busy you are, and they are communicating with you about how much they miss you, you are able to find a compromise on both issues. When I am with my kids I am not on my phone; I am with them one hundred percent.

Setting Up Your Office

Setting up your office is an exciting time, whether you work at a business, have a separate office, or work from home. When it comes to owning your own business, and setting up your office, you should try to arrange everything in a manner that makes it easier on you, and helps you complete tasks efficiently.

Furniture is a must when setting up your office, but where you set up that furniture can make a huge difference. Since you'll be spending so much time in your office, you want to ensure that your desk is in a place that you will be happy with. Speaking of sitting, you will also want to purchase a chair that you can handle sitting in for a lengthy period of time. Avoid the cheap plastic chair just because you see a good price tag.

Find something you can be happy with, and something that will be comfortable to sit in. Back problems are something you do not want years down the road, so making the investment now is worth it!

When organizing your office, you want to have all your filing cabinets and important items close enough to the desk that you are not stretching or having to move all around the room any time you need something.

When looking for furniture to include in your office, do not just look at the function side of it. Yes, you need items that will fit all the necessary tools and trinkets for your business, but you also need to enjoy walking into the space. Buy items that are both nice to look at, and have a reason to be purchased. If you need a shelf, get a shelf that fits all your papers, but also is something that you can handle looking at and are happy with.

Not only do you need to have furniture that you are happy with, you also want the background of the office to look the way you want it to look. So many times, you walk into an office and see that typical white or grey colour that looks drab and can make you want to put your head on your desk. Instead of that same old boring look, add some pops of colour to your office to get it looking bright and modern. Find a colour that has you walking into the room feeling energized and ready to start your day; it can make such a difference!

Lastly, it's a good idea for you to gain some knowledge about the technology you will be using in your office. Learn how to work with it so that it benefits you and doesn't frustrate you. Not only should you learn how to use the technology, you should also find a way to organize it. Avoid having cords and printers all over the place, so you are looking at them all day. Have them tucked away so you can focus on the important parts of the business.

An office is the place you want to go and feel at ease and ready to work. The last thing you need is stress over the little things. Now, time to get that office looking beautiful and ready to go!

Taking Action

Taking action is an important step for every person looking to start a business. Many times, we have ideas, but we have trouble sticking to them and actually putting them into action. However, to make a business successful, we need to hunker down and get the work done.

The first step is to push through the fear that you feel inside. Fear is something that stops a lot of us from pushing through and succeeding. You fear that something may fall through, so you avoid trying at all. However, to make your business a success you need to push through the fear and believe in yourself. Eventually, your confidence will shine through and you will no longer fear the thought of something failing. You will try because you know that nothing will happen if zero attempt is made.

Next, you should write up a daily, or even weekly, action plan. Sometimes when we look at the big picture, it is hard to see how we can get to the finish line. It is hard to start when the end seems so far away. This is why daily lists are important to help you focus. Instead of seeing all the work that has to be done, you are just focusing on one small task at a time, which in the end makes it easier to complete. There is no reason to get yourself overwhelmed, just take it one step at a time.

When you do start feeling overwhelmed, it is a good idea to have someone on your side. You want somebody you can go to when the day is tough and you need support. Your "go-to" person may be a friend, family member, or a business coach, but no matter who they are, they should be able to relieve stress when the day has just been too hard.

They can have you step away, and can give you a new perspective when you are feeling stuck. Find someone you trust because, while you may think you can do it all on your own, you need others to have your back when you are struggling to figure out your next move.

There is no reason to fear the unknown. Write out a plan, and take it day by day. Do not worry about all the little things. Eventually, they will all fall into place. Taking action is the biggest step you can take when starting a business, because it means you are moving forward instead of standing still. Even when you feel like giving up, keep moving forward and you will not regret it!

Chapter 3

Getting Started

"If opportunity doesn't knock, build a door."
– Milton Berle

The Techy Stuff

Learning a new skill, or changing your path in life in general can be hard, especially when having to take the first step. It is the fear of the unknown that often prevents us from trying new things. We fear that trying something different will cause everything in our life, whether it be personal or workplace-related, to fall apart.

However, with business, change is necessary to grow. Implementing new forms of technology is what helps grow your business, and helps it be what you have always imagined. To be successful in your business, you need to learn to adapt.

Technology is ever-changing. Within a year, it can be unrecognizable, which means it is up to you as the business owner to keep up with it and find ways to blend it into your business. Technology is not only important for yourself; it is also important for your client base or customers. It catches people's attention and gets them curious as to what you have to offer.

If you avoid keeping up with technology, your business can end up falling into the background because other companies were able to take that next step and keep their business modern and fresh.

You are most likely not alone in feeling like constant new technology can be overwhelming; however, technology is only overwhelming if you let it be. To avoid this feeling, try making it a regular part of your life; not just the business side. Adding technology into daily life makes you understand that it really isn't anything to fear, and is something you can easily learn as long as you have the passion and drive to do so.

Try focusing on the benefits that technology can offer you. It can greatly speed up your day, help you with tasks, and keep your customers happy. Even a modernized website can make a world of difference. Using social media and other online resources is something that can grow your customer base. Businesses that are still avoiding using the Internet as a resource are causing their company to fall into the background.

Businesses that keep up with the newest ways of communicating are most likely to gain new customers and even expand the age range for their customers since they are putting their business onto several platforms. Instead of flyers, use email, or create a website. There is always a way to bring technology into the business side of your life without feeling completely overwhelmed.

If you are unsure of where to start, try familiarizing yourself with the different forms of technology that are out there, and what they have to offer you. Take a look at different websites, blogs, or other platforms that share information about what is happening in the world of technology. While you may not need every resource that is out there, you will learn a lot, and find the types of tech you do need.

Not only can looking over different tech sites help you decide what is right for you, it can also offer you free trials. A lot of the time, the new forms of tech give free trials (usually thirty days) to let you see if it is something that could be used within your business. This gives you the opportunity to try the options out there, but without the commitment. Technology can be pricey, so any free trials are helpful when starting your business.

Technology is a wonderful thing. If used properly, it can help grow your business and get you to the next level. Looking back twenty years, technology is not at all the same as it once was. Despite that being the case, it is still quite simple to get used to and keep up with. If you are looking to grow your business, implementing that "techy stuff" can be the change you have been looking for!

Savings vs Debt

If you have debt, it can be difficult to think about anything else, especially putting money away for savings. Having to juggle the two can be quite stressful, but there are ways to decide what is best depending on your own personal situation. Each individual is different, and so are their financial situations, so it really depends on where you are at financially when it comes to deciding what to focus on more.

Saving money should always be in the back of your mind. It is necessary for your future, because you never know what could happen, and it is important to have an emergency fund set in place. As an example, let's say your car broke down. This car is what you use for work, and what helps you see clients. Well, clearly that car needs to be repaired to keep your business running efficiently.

If you have no savings, the money for the repairs has to come from somewhere, and most likely it is from a credit card or loan which is going to increase your debt. This is why having money put away is important no matter who you are, or what business you have.

However, saving can be tricky, especially when starting a business, so it's important to look at these factors when deciding on your savings being priority:

- Having no emergency savings whatsoever
- Having debt, but with a very low interest rate
- Having credit cards with not much owing on them

If your situation looks a lot like this, especially if you have no emergency money put aside, look towards getting at least an emergency fund. Hard times come up no matter who you are, and it is crucial to have back-up money just in case. You never know what could happen, and it is better to be prepared.

When it comes to focusing on debt repayment, you have to look at how much debt you have, and the amount of interest you are paying on it. If you are paying a high interest rate, it is important to start getting those payments made, because the longer you hold off, the more you will end up paying in the long run.

If you have several different types of debt, you should look at all of the amounts you owe, and the interest rate of each, in order to decide which to focus on first, and what to pay on each loan or debt. Once that is established, you can create a monthly budget that can help you stay focused with your repayment. In many cases, paying off debt is of highest importance.

However, as mentioned above, if there is no emergency savings, get that established first so that you have a backup plan. Then, focus on your debt so you can get that stress eliminated and move on to saving for your future and/or your business.

The best solution would be fitting both savings and debt repayment into your life. If you can find a balance between the two, that gives you the best long-term result. You can slowly pay off your debt while also putting money away into savings. It gives you a chance to avoid debt taking over, but also gives you a backup plan in case something comes up and you have to put money towards it.

Finding Time for Yourself

The routine of daily life can take a toll on anyone, especially when you are running a business. It can be difficult to find time just to relax and get back to feeling like your normal self. No matter how busy your schedule is, though, you should take time to do something you enjoy, and something that makes you feel both happy and refreshed.

Finding time for yourself gives you time to reboot your brain, and gives yourself a chance in the long term to become more productive. While you may feel like a superhero, the human brain cannot handle a constant flood of information, and focus for a lengthy period of time without taking at least a small break for yourself. Me time gives you the refresh you need, and you will realize that even a small bit of time for yourself can get you ready to continue with your day and keep your focus at full capacity.

"Me time" gives you a better balance between work and your personal life. It gives you the option to say, "No, I think I have done enough today," and step away from the stress for a brief moment. Taking on every task that comes your way may feel like a good thing because you are getting that long list checked off, but remembering to manage your time, and not do everything at once, will help you to feel less drained at the end of the day.

If you avoid taking those breaks, you never have that moment to recharge your batteries. You will not only have higher amounts of stress, but you will also feel tired, achy, and all around just not good.

Taking time for yourself also can help improve concentration because you are not giving your brain tons of information all throughout the day. Your mind does not always do well under pressure, and avoiding breaks will surely get you feeling frazzled by bedtime. An energized brain can do a lot more than a tired-out brain can, so give it the rest it needs!

Having time to spend with yourself will also help you discover who you truly are. While it may seem silly to say, spending time by yourself, listening to your own thoughts and opinions, can do wonders for your health in general. Mentally, you can discover things you never knew about yourself, which can benefit you both in your personal life and your business life.

You can also take time to figure out your goals in life, and how you see your future. Throughout the day, we are usually asked a million questions, or have an endless list of tasks to accomplish. Very rarely do we spend time with ourselves, asking the serious questions and figuring out what truly would make us happy. Me time allows that to happen, and can allow you to think hard about the path you are on, and whether or not you are headed in the right direction.

Time for yourself is not only important for you, it is also important for the people around you. Your relationships are affected (whether you see it or not) when you are stressed, and just not feeling like yourself. If you are not feeling good about yourself, then it is hard to work on the relationships you have in your life. Properly caring for yourself means that you can care for the people who matter most to you!

Now that you know why it is important to have time for yourself, you need to sort out what your "me time" looks like. This can really be anything, but it should be something you truly enjoy, and that makes you feel good to be putting time into. If you have kids, it could be spending time at the park with them; it doesn't necessarily need to be completely by yourself.

Here are some ideas just to get your mind flowing:

- Journaling
- Watching your favourite show
- Reading a book
- Being out in nature

Take full advantage of whatever it is that makes you happy, and see the difference it makes in your life.

Growing Emotionally and Professionally

You might believe that, once you reach a certain age, you no longer experience any growth. Well, it's time to throw that thought out the window, and be aware that any age is time for growth, both emotionally and professionally. Throughout our lives, we learn new things, we experience new things, and we go through a multitude of different up and down emotions. We are meant to keep experiencing life and growing through those experiences.

Without growth, we would stay the same individuals from roughly age twenty and up, and you and I both know that just does not happen.

The person you were in your twenties is not going to be the person you are in your forties. Through failures and successes, you learn who you are, and what works best for you. You learn how to move past difficult times, and express yourself in a way that reflects who you are as an individual.

Living life is all about discovering who you truly are, and what you want in your future. As you get older, what you want in your future definitely becomes clearer, but it does not stop you from growing as a person; that growth is inevitable and necessary for you to enjoy your life to the fullest.

To help you grow both professionally and emotionally, you need to be able to open your mind and your heart to the possibilities that are out there. You need to see that you are not stuck in a certain way, and you always have the ability to make adjustments in who you are, what you do, and/or how you express yourself. You are capable of bettering yourself each and every day, and all it takes is reflecting and knowing you have the strength to change any parts of your life or yourself that you feel are in need of adjustment.

While some changes in your life are not under your control, you do have the control to grow and move past the difficult moments that you had no control over. If you felt out of control in regards to your divorce, or even starting a new life, you can take that control back and realize you are the one who can change both how you feel, and how you live your days. Do not give up just because you do not see growth as a possibility. Growth can happen to anyone, as long as they open their arms up to accept it, and put in the effort to make it happen.

Be Proud

The dictionary definition of proud is: Feeling deep pleasure or satisfaction as a result of one's own achievements, qualities or possessions of those of someone with whom one is closely associated.

This is something I've struggled with, not only in business but in my personal life. I've always been proud of my children, and I tell them how proud I am on a regular basis. However, I don't often recognize the things in me and my business that I should be proud of. I've tried to improve, and I've learned that if you are proud of what you do, the product or service you create, then you can only get better from there.

I know this can be a common struggle for people as it is easier to tell others what they are good at, and the amazing things they are doing, than it is to tell yourself. As human beings, we are used to looking at our faults, and what we can improve upon instead of seeing the good we are already doing. It is common to focus on the negative instead of the positive, and no matter who you are, or what stage you are in within your own life, you should feel proud about where you are, and the steps you are taking in your life.

No matter the length of time, or the effort it may take to get yourself to where you want to be, every small step is something worth celebrating and being proud of. The more you take notice of all those small moments of success, the more you will start to feel proud of yourself, and see the wonderful changes you are making.

So, how can you work on being proud of yourself? Well, to start with, you can try and take the time each and every day to give yourself a pat on the back for something good you did that day. While they may seem small, they are successes that add to the vision you have set in your mind. They are the stepping stones to the finish line.

In my personal life, and my business, I have had my fair share of moments where I feel down on myself, or regret the choices I have made. In those moments, though, I keep reminding myself that there is a much bigger picture involved, and not every day is going to be perfect, nor will I feel like everything is falling perfectly into place. There are natural ups and downs in life, and despite what happens, it is important to always strive to look at the good and focus on the parts of your life that make you feel proud and keep moving you forward.

Chapter 4

Business and Personal Balance

"It's all about quality of life and finding a happy balance between work and friends and family."
– Philip Green

Finding Balance

Being balanced gives you the feeling of calmness. It makes you feel like you are at ease and clear headed to keep going with the daily stressors that life brings you. It means you are not becoming too overwhelmed in every aspect of your life, and you have the motivation to accomplish all your wants and needs.

Finding balance is important because, without it, you can feel anxious and unsure about the next steps to take, or even the direction in which to head. Daily goals can be harder to accomplish, and even simple things you're used to, such as work, can start becoming too much to handle. If you are overwhelmed and are lacking balance, it can show up in every part of your life, which of course you want to avoid.

Finding balance is not as hard as one may think. It just takes some time and motivation to figure out what the problem is, and how to solve it. If you are having difficulty in balancing your life, it is usually caused by focusing on one thing more than everything else.

If you focus on just work, and not your personal life whatsoever, then you are not focusing on all the needs you have. No matter who you are, personal or "me time" is a must. You need that break away from the stressors to truly feel like yourself again.

To find some balance in your life, you need to start by taking a good look at your life, and all the things on that lengthy to do list that you keep in your head constantly. Take a look at all you do, and how it makes you feel. It is important to put an emotion to each task to get an understanding as to what is causing the most stress.

You need to also take a look at what parts of your life you are not focusing on. This for most people is their personal life. Usually, people tend to focus on the things that they think need to get done. Cleaning and work become first priority, which is great, but you need to remember that doing things just for you and pampering yourself is important for your own well-being.

If you do too much, you end up drained, and cannot focus on the parts in your life that you deemed most important to begin with. This is why you need to balance everything out and make sure you incorporate time for you into your daily life.

Once you have established what parts of your life you are not focusing on as much as you probably should, you need to start setting goals for yourself, and getting you back to your usual self! Setting goals gives you an outline on what to do, and when to do it. It gives you a timeline to help you stay on track and be successful.

Start making a list, and create tasks, whether they are daily, weekly, monthly, or even yearly. Keep them somewhere visible to remind you every day. While you may not immediately start focusing on the parts of your life you have been avoiding, you will eventually want to do so, because you are giving yourself reminders everywhere of the importance of caring for yourself.

You know yourself best, so if there are things you know you tell yourself when you are trying to avoid a certain task, jot that down, and even put a sticky note somewhere telling yourself to ignore those thoughts, and that you do matter. Do not get in the way of yourself, or push yourself off track. Instead, keep yourself motivated and tell yourself you matter enough to find that balance.

Lastly, remember to be kind to yourself. If you find you are losing balance again, do not let it get you down. Just pick yourself back up again and keep moving. Life is filled with stressors, and there is no reason to add more stress to it by giving yourself heck for not following through. It will happen, and you just need to remember that you are important. Everything will fall into place, and balance will come with time. You will get there.

Don't Just Think About It

Overthinking is one of those things that everyone does at one time or another. It is when you think about something, and then get stuck in your head because you are so fixated on it. Sometimes, when we overthink things, we end up not taking action because the thinking is keeping us occupied and unable to make an actual decision. This is something that should be avoided because we can end up with thoughts spinning around, but with nothing actually being done about it.

To turn an idea into an action, you need to have the motivation and drive to move past the thought stage. Staying in your head and thinking about the million things you want to do in your life is great, but it doesn't actually get you to that point, only taking action can.

When trying to move past the thinking phase, and into doing, you need to make a plan and stick to it. If you have an idea, think about how you can turn it into an action. Get off your feet and get moving. Staying in your head may feel comforting, but it is a menace in disguise as it tricks you into thinking you have actually taken a step forward. An idea only becomes something more when you put effort into it and turn it into reality.

Having your thoughts become a reality will make you feel confident about yourself, and feeling like you can take on the world. Start by being a thinker, but make that thought something real so you became a doer instead!

Choose Action, Not Reaction

As a single mom and entrepreneur, I had to learn to be more proactive and less reactive. When I first became a single mom, everything I did was reactive. Not just with my home life but with my business too. Something always had to be done, so I just became reactive to what was on fire in any given moment.

If I had a deadline, often I'd be up all night to meet that deadline because my day was constantly interrupted and I couldn't get it done during the day. I also had a hard time saying no to anyone. If I received an email, I answered it; if the kids needed me, I was there. In the end I was letting everyone down, even myself.

I learned that schedules matter, and now every hour of my day is in my daily planner that sits on my desk.

I also learned that I can say no, and I can schedule tasks into a later time and date. When I say I schedule everything, I mean everything. From what client I am working on, walking the dog, grocery shopping, even me time is scheduled. If it's not in the schedule it just doesn't happen. My schedule is my lifeline to success, both personally and professionally.

I also learned that when the phone rings or someone comes to the door, I keep working. I was so afraid of letting people down that I was letting everyone down. There will always be exceptions but not everything can be an exception.

When I started keeping to my wonderful schedule (the Daily Planner by Shelagh Cummins), I also started feeling like I was accomplishing something. If it was in my planner I never missed an invoice or an appointment.

As time went on I was even able to over-deliver; if it was due on the fifteenth, I could have it done on the tenth. I started to take action and I was doing less reacting. This also meant less stress, a happier me, happier clients and a happier family. I was able to fit more time in for dog walking, time with the kids, and me as well!

Confidence

Confidence gives you the drive to keep pushing, even on the toughest of days. If you lack confidence, it can affect how you do things, and how you feel throughout the day. It can affect your work, relationships, and your health. Having confidence is what can help you reach that point of success in your life that you have been dreaming of, and that is just the start.

The benefits of having self-confidence are endless, but here are some just to give you an idea:

- Healthier relationships
- Less stress
- Better performance
- Higher energy
- More open to try new things

If you are looking to boost your self-confidence, there are some tips that can help you along the way. To start with, taking care of your body can really improve your confidence. If you haven't been eating properly, or exercising on a regular basis, you may be feeling a little down on yourself.

If you are struggling, try taking it one step at a time. Each day, do something positive for your body. Something that makes you feel good at the end of the day and has you feeling ready to start the next day. Eventually, these small steps will get you back to feeling like you are in the body you love, and your confidence will start shining through.

While starting this journey of self-confidence, you need to remember not to be so hard on yourself. Big changes do not happen in a day. Things take time, and that is okay. No matter how long it may take to get your confidence back, you need to continue to be kind to yourself, and understand that with time, good things will come.

When looking at ways to be kind to yourself, positive self-talk is a great option. Self-talk is the thoughts you tell yourself either out loud, or in your head. With positive self-talk, you want to tell yourself things that make you feel good about yourself. You can do this in front of a mirror, or even just lying in bed thinking to yourself.

A lot of the time, we tell ourselves negative things. We tell ourselves what we should have done instead of thinking about what we did right. Instead of saying "I shouldn't have done that today," tell yourself something you did do that made you happy, or made you feel good. There is no reason to bring yourself down when you have the opportunity to bring yourself up!

If you are still struggling to increase your confidence, try finding people in your life who make you feel good about yourself. Being around positive people can change the way you think and feel. Positivity is both addictive and contagious. If everyone around you is positive and happy, you will want to feel that too, and that will bring your confidence up for sure!

However, do not feel down about the people around you. If your loved ones or other people in your life are in a different stage than you in their life, do not let that bring you down. Comparing yourself to everyone around you does no good. It causes you to question your own choices in life, when your choices were made for you and you only. Everyone is different, and that includes their life. Be happy about where you are in your life, and stop worrying about where everyone else is.

If you are unsure of where to start, below are some self-care tips you can do to help boost your confidence:

- Making sure you are getting proper sleep
- Taking a look at your diet to start focusing on eating healthier
- Trying meditation to get yourself focused on you and what matters
- Exercising on a regular basis
- Finding an activity that makes you feel happy (hiking, drawing, singing, etc.)

Do not let a lack of confidence take over your life. Find the things you enjoy, and get back to feeling confident about yourself. It may be a journey to get back to feeling fully confident, but it is a journey worth travelling.

Office Hours Required

Working from home can have its challenges, and some people think that because you work from home you can accommodate their schedule, not matter what it is. And yes, sometimes this is true, but if I take an hour out for a coffee or a visit at 10am, I have to add that hour to my day. This often leads to some very late nights and weekends.

For years I did this, then one day the light bulb went off. "Office hours required!" It was that easy. I put in office hours, I told my family and friends that unless it was an emergency or a scheduled event my office hours were 8am – 6pm. Why didn't I think of this sooner?

I was constantly playing catch-up because I stopped for this person or that, or I took a personal phone call. I felt overwhelmed and at the end of the day when I should have been packing it in for some time with my kids I was just starting my day. I thought that, because I worked at home, office hours didn't make sense, but the reality is that they make perfect sense ... and they work!! Learn from my mistakes along the way, and start with office hours. Don't be afraid to send out an email or post on your office door. Some people may be upset in the beginning, but they will come around and you will have a better life work balance.

I became an entrepreneur to control my destiny, so I had to take the control back, even if it hurt a few people along the way.

Dating Again

I originally was not going to include this topic, as my own experience with it has been dismal. Having said that, I felt I wasn't alone and that I should include my experiences.

I was the mature age of forty-nine when I went back into the dating scene. I had been married just shy of ten years, and had dated my ex-husband for a few years prior to marriage. I was amazed at how things had changed.

Not only had the dating scene changed, but I, and my life, had changed a lot too. I had matured, had become very independent, and had a few extra pounds on me that I was self-conscious about. But here is the thing, I now had no time to date; I was a businesswomen, and a mom, and I was doing it all alone.

So where exactly would I fit dating into this scenario? I always felt the most loneliness around the holidays and longed to share them with someone. I pushed my feelings out of the way, convincing myself I was fine without someone to love.

My friends would push me and say, "Do online dating" or "Get out there!" Often late at night when the kids were at their dad's and I was in the house alone, it would hit me the most. I missed the simple things: conversation, laughs, snuggles, just feeling the closeness of a relationship.

Online dating was painful for me; profile up, profile down, picture up, picture down. I would view profiles but never respond or meet anyone. Then my friend Shannon said, "JUST DO IT!!" So I did. This was early on, and I was still carrying the baggage of divorce. I went on two dates. One crashed and burned, and one was affected by a language barrier. I was convinced that everyone I spoke to was an axe murderer, and I just couldn't go this route. Shannon suggested that if I wanted go on a successful online date I needed to watch less CSI.

But of course, late at night when I was feeling the need to speak to an adult I would try it again. After my first experience with online dating I never went out with anyone again. I grew up with a very loving family and my parents were married just shy of 60 years when my dad passed away. I watched my mom struggle the years after Dad was taken from us as she was missing a piece of herself. They had what I always wished for, true love. They had their ups and downs over the years but they loved each other wholeheartedly and it showed.

So why couldn't I find this? What was wrong with me? Truthfully It wasn't me; I was born in a generation of meeting in real life and this new online dating was a struggle for me. Who was real and who wasn't? I am not an athlete and it seemed everyone I looked at was climbing Mount Everest for shits and giggles. I wanted to spend my Saturday night with a glass of wine, a bonfire and someone special.

The moral of my story: I tried, and every once in a while, I may try again. I am still hesitant meeting people in real life from a dating app but I can check it off as I made the effort. But I also learned to take risks, safe ones. That guy you meet while walking the dog, stop and talk to him, get to know him. I needed to find my comfort zone in the new world of dating, and you can too. I also had to convince myself that nice guys do exist. I learned that you can be friendly and cautious when you are looking to meet the right person.

In order to keep me and my family safe, I always met at a coffee shop, and never divulged my address until I had known someone for a while. I was overly cautious when it came to meeting up with people. I met some great people along the way and I even met someone who restored my faith in kindness, and has since become one of my best friends. My feelings are: the one that will stand out from the crowd is probably that person right in your backyard; you just never knew it.

I've learned that making time to date is not the waste of time I once thought it was. That not everyone has a hidden agenda, you just need to get to know them. That maybe if nothing else you'll find a new best friend. That no matter how busy you are, if you want it to happen you will mutually be able to make it happen.

Juggling work and kids' schedules on both sides, it seems like there is never time, but there actually is. I went from working seven days a week to keeping one day every other week for me. Should I find the true love I am looking for one day, then we will work out more time for each other, together.

What you want is very important, so don't do anything you're not comfortable with. If he cares about you and you find a love connection, he will respect you enough to understand you too.

I separated in 2005 and I still haven't found the right person. I am okay with that; I am not in a rush, my kids come first, and one day I may or may not find someone but I am allowing myself the opportunity.

Your soulmate is out there. Don't put a clock on it, don't get discouraged, and don't give up. Figure out the best style of dating for you, and one day your true love will be standing right in front of you.

Health and Fitness

This is a chapter that I of all people should not be writing, but I am going to do so with a spin. I'm going to write not about how to get healthy, but my own struggles with getting healthy. The day my brother passed away from cancer at the young age of 59 is a day I will never forget. My brother was the image of perfect health. He went to the gym, and he ate well, for the most part. We all need treats and his was chocolate chip cookies. I used to bake them for him when we were young, and then my daughter baked them for him and delivered in most recent years.

When I looked at my brother I used to wish I had the same dedication to my health as he did. And then it happened; he got an illness, and how healthy he was didn't matter. But the truth is we were blessed to have him a year longer than expected due to him being in such great health. And although I was angry when my big brother was taken from us far too soon, I realized that I needed to make some changes in my life.

Pregnancy and I were not friends; I was very sick, and almost left this earth with both my kids. I went into severe shock with one, and cardiac arrest with the other. I was always small prior to having children, but having gestational diabetes with both caused me to pack on the pounds. Losing the weight afterwards was a constant struggle, and my sweet tooth for chocolate when I am stressed did not help one bit. I'd never been on a diet in my life and here I was feeling uncomfortable in my own skin. I was that young girl that everyone hated because I could eat anything and not put a pound on.

I was always mostly a healthy eater, so this part was easy for me, but exercise on a regular routine was my struggle. I could eat carrot sticks for a month and be fine with it, but to get into a gym or find the time to exercise at home was very hit and miss. One day here then one day next month. Working the hours I was working early on, I would be so tired when I shut down my computer that I was done.

The first thing I did was get a dog, for both my emotional and physical self. I ended up with the most loving dog a person could ask for, and he is my best friend. He also tells me when it's walk time. I have exercise equipment in my house but it seemed to be a great clothes rack and I never really did much more with it. I decided to figure out why these expensive clothes racks never got used. It was mostly location; I had to pull them out to use them. So I found places in the house that worked.

I guess what I am getting at is, in order to stay active, you need to make it easy for yourself.

Here are a few pointers that will help you stay on track with your health and fitness:

Keep Track – No matter how tired you feel after that workout, track your progress to let yourself know how well you are doing. It is great to look back and see all the improvements you have made. It boosts your self-esteem and also makes you feel more motivated to keep going!

Drink Water – It may seem like drinking water cannot really make much of a difference. However, drinking water not only improves your hydration, it also improves your mood, skin, and increases energy. The more you drink, the better you will start to feel.

Lose the Loose Clothing – I know in some ways you may think it can help looking at all the clothes that are now too big for you, and in some ways, it can boost your mood a little. Despite how good you may feel looking at the old clothes, it is only a reminder of your past. When you are trying to move forward and create a whole new lifestyle for yourself, leave the past where it belongs so you can focus on the new.

Make Fitness Fun – When you avoid bringing the fun into fitness, it can deter you from wanting to continue. Instead of doing the same old activities, try switching it up. Do something you have never tried before. It gets you to try new things, and also keeps you moving at the same time.

Chapter 5

Networking and Marketing

"Networking has been cited as the number one unwritten rule of success in business. Who you know really impacts what you know."
– Sallie Krawcheck

Friends and Family

Every new business starts with family and friends. Once you've made the decision, you'll be excited, so don't keep it a secret; it's time to tell the world. Spend some time over the next while telling everyone. Don't listen to the naysayers, and they will be out there, drown them out with your excitement. Call up your friends and family and tell them, "I am the business owner of... ...". Be excited and proud that you're starting this business. If you are having a launch party, be sure to let them know.

Think of yourself as screaming to everyone from the mountain tops, picture it in your head, dancing through the streets yelling, "I am the new business owner of ..." These visions in your head will keep you smiling as you call up everyone you know and tell them you are excited, and that you need their support. It's time for you to take control of your world, and you need them to help you start on your journey.

Tell them exactly what you need. Maybe it is just emotional support, but maybe you need more. If you are opening an administrative business, (bookkeeping, virtual assistance, etc), you may need a little extra help. Do you need some help to set up an office? Then ask!

Nobody can help you if you don't ask. I know better than anyone, as I am famous for this one. I am always there to help, but I suck at asking for help. But I am working on it. Lay it out word for word what you need. Maybe a family member has a desk you could use, or time they can supply to help get your office set up.

If you are thinking about a bricks and mortar location that will take a lot more investment, but now is the best time to do it and start making positive changes; not tomorrow, not next week. . . now! You're already transitioning to your new life, so why not continue the transition with something that makes you happy? Just make sure you ask your family the hard questions, such as, "Can you donate some time to assist me to start my new business?" or "I would love if you'd spend the day with me to help me build my dreams."

Do not let your family's negativity hold you back, only move forward with those that are happy and excited for you. If I had listened to everyone that told me to get a "real job," I would not be where I am today.

As I continued on my entrepreneurial journey, I paid my mortgage with the money from my business, and as things began to grow, all the naysayers realized I wasn't crazy after all. I did have what it takes to become a successful entrepreneur. You can make your own success; you just need to want it, and want it so bad that it becomes your other child.

It has always amazed me how my kids can be my best marketers. We sometimes forget the people they meet, the friends that have parents that may need your services, the coach; the list goes on and on. How many times have we not even thought about the network our kids have for us? I am not saying push your kids to sell your services, but rather to realize the resources you have around you, and the connections that you have.

I had never thought of this route before, but one day I was chatting with my daughter and she expressed that one of her friends' moms was interested in a product I was selling at the time. It got me to thinking about all the other connections I had made through my kids and the programs they attend, such as my son's coach. Every business needs a bookkeeper, so why not me?

Local Businesses

I live in a small community of just forty-five thousand, and growing. I know many of the business owners by their name, and I consider myself lucky because of this. Whether you live in a small or a large community, businesses want to help fellow businesses. It's like most clubs; we are like-minded individuals wanting to succeed. For that reason, you can build your network with other local businesses.

There may be an option to cross-promote each other depending on what your businesses are. Everywhere I go there is a potential new client until they say no, and then that is just no today. You never know what the future may hold!

When I think of local business I also think of the local Chamber of Commerce. My local chamber is exceptional. However, do not just join. Instead, become known in your chamber. My schedule doesn't allow for me to go to a lot of the events, but I make a point of staying up to date, and I take advantage of networking and promotional items they have made available.

I've been a member of my chamber for many years with different businesses, and not only have they opened doors for me, they have also assisted in media promotions.

When I first started and didn't have a lot of time for marketing, they assisted in that area, which helped me greatly!

There are also many networking groups locally for your niche. Research and find out what's out there. If nothing exists, start a local networking group for business owners. Connecting with other business owners is essential in my opinion. Some have already been through the struggles and can help, and some are going through struggles you have personally been through and can assist you in some way. Sharing knowledge is always good, provided it's a two-way street, and some secrets may remain yours if necessary.

Hiring a Professional

I've spoken about finding the right coach for you and your business in a previous chapter but I want to talk about hiring other professionals to assist you. It can be a difficult decision, especially when you are so used to doing things on your own, and not getting any assistance. For most, it can be hard to fully let go of those reins and feel like you can trust someone to assist in making decisions, or at least assist you in the advice side of making those important decisions.

Something I've always told my clients is to "do what you're good at and hire for the rest." But I was not good at taking my own advice for a very long time. My business coach would tell me I needed to let go, I needed to stop working so much, but I was afraid to do this since I had always handled every aspect of my business, and some weeks that meant working 24 hours a day 7 days a week. It was not unusual for me to work until the sun came up. My neighbours knew when I was working around the clock because when they left for work in the early morning hours my lights would still be on from the night before. This was going to result in burnout, and everyone around me was telling me so.

Then one day it hit me, it was time. I was overworked and overwhelmed, and the business was continuing to grow but I was burning out. My starting point for the big changes in my business was with a coach. Coaches exist for a very good reason; they specialize in different aspects of someone's life, so while you may find a coach who can assist you in all areas of your life, this can be hard to come by, and a lot of the time, it can help seeing what other professionals or coaches have to offer, and how it may benefit your life and/or business.

Having said that, I have had the same business coach for many, many years and I would not change that. She has even assisted me in making the professional contacts I required to further assist my business. She helped me build my network and my team. Professionals can assist you where you need it, when you need it. You just have to find the right fit.

Although your list of professionals will most likely be very different from mine, here are a few from my list of professionals:

- Website
- Marketing
- Social media
- Bookkeepers and accountants
- and of course, Coaches

Although I am still the "main" bookkeeper in my business and oversee all my clients, having someone with experience that complements my own expertise has been a game changer in my business. It wasn't just about the experience; it also had to be someone that I could work with, and with whom I connected.

Putting the right professionals in place in your business can make the difference in not only your life and your health, but also the success of your business. While your business coach will push you to move forward, keep you feeling proud of the steps you are taking in your life, and the good you are doing for yourself and your business, they will also guide you with the right professionals to include as part of your business.

While you may believe you can do it all on your own, and I am sure you can, a professional is a great way to go to when you just need that extra assistance to keep your business going. They are not there to take away from you in any way, but to assist you and the growth of your business. That first step to hiring professionals in your business and letting go is the hardest, but most likely one of the best decisions you will make with your coach. For me it was the fear of the extra financial burden, but now when I look back I don't know why I didn't do it sooner. If you find the right people to put in place, the results are rewarding.

Marketing

My strengths are in my ability to be a good bookkeeper, to see outside of the box, and properly assist my clients. I am educated in bookkeeping and my qualifications are in bookkeeping; however, I am not a marketer. So how do I market my business without the experience to do so?

This is a tough one in the beginning, as the money is not always there to hire someone, but you can do more harm by marketing your business improperly, so it is important to be careful and make sure if you are marketing, that it is the right way.

We all have digital media linked to our business, so that is the only marketing I do. Even with that it's sparse. I generally hire someone to do any other marketing for me. Why? The answer is simply that I am not good at it. Know your strengths and hire for your weaknesses. We are all good at something, and that is where we should focus.

My best marketing has been word of mouth. Lucky for me, my business has been built on my reputation and word of mouth, and this allows for my phone to ring with new business, and I close the deal.

Even though I am not good at marketing, I still take courses, and go to events that teach marketing skills. To be a good entrepreneur, you want to be familiar with, and aware of, all aspects of your business but still focus on what you do best.

Networking

What is a network and where does it come from? It is a group of people that can potentially come from every person you've ever talked to throughout your lifetime. I have had a few different businesses in my lifetime, and I've met many people. When I first started, I had books and books of businesses cards; I still actually have these today. Now, most of my "database" is on some kind of computerized database.

Putting yourself out there and starting a business from the ground up can be overwhelming to think about, let alone having to actually take action and make it a reality. Networking is a way you can let people know about your business, and how you communicate once you get that business. It can make or break your business if you do not take the right steps, or get the right types of advertising out for the world to see.

Networking is all about how you interact with future clients, or even present ones. It is growing your business through communication with others who can help you. If you need new clients or customers coming in the door, networking with people who can put your brand out there through various avenues is a great way to make that happen!

You can network in many different ways, whether it be going to different business networking events to find like-minded people who could help grow your business, or even conferences for something that would benefit your business; you never know who you can meet when you put yourself out there, which is why networking is a must have in any business.

Here are a few different types of networking just to help you get started:

Personal Networking – this type of networking is finding people outside of your business who are like-minded individuals and can help you grow your business, or your knowledge. They could even be people who own businesses similar to yours. It is all about exchanging information with people who are on a similar path, and picking at their brain a little bit to see what can be improved upon either personally, or in your business.

Operational Networking – this form of networking is the opposite of Personal Networking. It is all about working alongside people within your company to help benefit the business, and help it grow. Communication is key in running a functioning company, so as a business owner, you need to constantly communicate with the people around you so that you know if everything is running smoothly, or if there are kinks that need to be smoothed out. You do not know unless you ask!

Strategic Networking – with this type of networking, you are using strategy to find people who can benefit your business the most. Once you know what you want, and how you want your business to grow, you start to get a better picture of who you need to be in contact with to make your business grow quickly and efficiently. Strategic Networking is going to the right people to get what you want out of your business.

While these types of networking are similar, they all have a different approach and different people you need to communicate with. A business runs smoothly when the right people are involved, and it is about figuring out who those people are.

Every time you meet a person or shake their hand, ask for their card, enter it into your database, and record a little note as a reminder of where you met this person, as well as key notes about the conversation. You are now building your network. You may wonder why because you may not think you need a contact for whatever type of business they may be in. While this may be true today, you may need them down the road, or better yet, they may need you.

Webpage/Digital Media

Creating your webpage, as well as your social and digital media, is a great way to expand your business, and get people of all groups and ages to start taking notice. Your business is your baby, and you should try and venture out into as many different avenues as you can to become known and get business coming in.

If you avoid taking the time to add in these parts of your business, then you are taking away all those chances of people taking notice. We are in a world of ever-changing technology, and while some still avoid it for different reasons, the majority of the population is very involved in the online world, and takes notice when a company knows how to brand themselves and represent themselves.

Creating your webpage and digital media is your chance to show everyone what you are all about and what your intentions are with your business. It is a way to put it all out there in regard to your business plan, what you offer, and how you view yourself as a business owner.

When you look at your webpage, it should scream your personality and your business so that people know the second they look at it who you are, and how your business can help them. Think about what you look for when searching on a website. What stands out to you? Even something as simple as the visuals of a webpage can make a huge difference because they show your type of branding and the type of clients your business caters to.

No matter what type of media you are creating for your business, it should be something you are proud to show, and something you would look at and immediately want to know more about. As good as your business is, it is all about how you make it stand out and get those clients in the door that makes all the difference!

Chapter 6

All About the Books

"Don't ever let your business get ahead of the financial side of your business. Accounting, accounting, accounting. Know your numbers."
– Tilman J. Fertitta

My Path to Bookkeeping

I want to share my journey with you in order to help you with your decision-making about the business that best suits you. It definitely helps if you're knowledgeable in the choice you make. You will want there to be a need for your service / product, and for me most importantly you need to enjoy what you're doing. This is my journey to my business.

In the late nineties, I took a job with an internet service provider as office manager.

The first day I arrived there was a copy of QuickBooks Desktop sitting on my desk. My job was to move the bookkeeping to a computerized version. I'd never used any bookkeeping software but I was well versed in Office products. Over the next few months, I learned it and used it successfully.

Because my dad was Vice President of Finance for a large company in Toronto, I asked him to assist me in an audit to ensure I was doing everything correctly. The best compliment I ever received was the praise from my dad about what an outstanding job I had done.

I stayed at this company for a few years, until I decided to go out on my own in the late nineties. I ran a horse boarding facility and I did bookkeeping out of the barn office during the day when the horses were out. I continued working with QuickBooks but felt I needed some training so I got my first certification in 2007 as a QuickBooks Desktop pro-advisor.

I decided to move back to the city and take a full-time job in the finance department of a large corporation. They taught me data bases and how to use SQL, and I spent the next few years in my position of data base management in the finance department. I excelled in this position and learned a lot about data bases, but little did I know this would help me in future years.

I was married in August 2005 and pregnant in September 2005. After my daughter was born and we had moved to a 10 acre farm an hour north of the city, I decided to leave my job in the city and stay home with my daughter and my horses. Shortly thereafter, I opened up Edmiston Office Services, which was more of a VA business that offered bookkeeping as well.

In 2008, my son was born and a short time after I opened a digital media business, I was working from the farm while my then husband was commuting to downtown Toronto. I did some bookkeeping on the side, but mostly focused my time on the digital media business. During this time, I also community produced and co-hosted a show on Rogers TV Georgina, and I even did some blogging for York-Scene. These were the years I was building my network, although I didn't realize it at the time.

January 2015, I closed the digital media business and in April of that same year my husband and I separated. Life was about to change in a very big way.

We had moved away from the farm by this time, and although we had stayed in the same town we were in a more central area. My ex had moved back to the city for a while until we sorted everything out, and there I was in town on my own, no job to speak of and two kids depending on me.

I had to find a place to live, a career path, deal with the divorce, my ex, lawyers, and do it all with a smile on my face. I took a few different bookkeeping jobs, and even some VA type jobs. The problem was the kids were still young and they were going through a lot, and working a full-time job just wasn't working out. Even with flex time I was struggling with the work / kid balance.

It was around this time I met who would be the landlord of my home over the next few years. Through this time I crossed the path of some great people. My landlord would be the first of many to assist me on getting on the path I needed to walk. Why was my landlord part of this? He took a chance on me. I didn't have the credit that looked good on paper at this time. I told him I wouldn't let him down, and he agreed to rent me the townhouse, and even today, this is someone I've never forgotten about, because he rented to me based on my work and not my financial background.

Over the next few years, I proved to him I was a woman of my word, and not once was my rent late. When he and his dad would come to fix things, we'd have some laughs and, although he might not have known, he lifted my spirits when I needed a break.

Now that I had a place to call home, I had to start building my business to move away from the various bookkeeping jobs I was doing. In a way my career path chose me.

In the words of my business coach, choose the path that you're good at and you enjoy. Bookkeeping was screaming my name. My business name changed from AB Plus K Virtual Business Services, to AB Plus K Virtual Bookkeeping Services.

My First Client

My first client came from a place I didn't expect. She is someone that I respect and feel grateful to have had in my life for many years. She knew me before my divorce; I met her at a conference from my previous business. I followed her on social media and attended her events. She took a chance on me. Although I'd had twenty years' experience as a bookkeeper, I had never jumped in with two feet as a full-time bookkeeper.

I needed to organize my business to be successful. She helped me do this, and then hired me to work for her as her corporate bookkeeper. This was and still is today, the toughest client I've ever had; not that the work is any more difficult, but I never want to let her down. In the beginning I would overthink this, and this was also a learning curve for me. I was not giving myself the credit that I deserved; I was and am I great bookkeeper, but I was going through a divorce and my confidence was not there. Through the ups and downs she has stayed with me. I am proud to be her bookkeeper, and I am happy she was my very first client.

I had to keep building though, so now it was off to client two. They found me on Facebook, where they had posted an ad for a bookkeeper. It was close to home so we started chatting and I went to meet them. I met with the two owners of the company at the time, as well as the bookkeeper. I was hired and I was on my way. They are still clients of mine today, and over the years we've formed a friendship. The guys at this shop have always looked out for me, and

I've looked out for them. Again, you never know where you find those to help you in your new life, the people that make you feel like you're not doing this alone.

I found these people in places I never expected, but I couldn't be the successful business woman I am today without these people touching my life, and supporting me along the way. These great people I met in the first year of starting over bought into me, not my resumé or credit rating.

Now that I had a home and a client, I was on my way. But one client was not going to build my business and support my family. It was time to do more. It was a tough few years building and marketing my business, and juggling the kids. But build a good name for yourself and the clients will come, then word of mouth will bring more and before you know it you will have a great client base.

Finding the Right Bookkeeper

Having a client base is not enough to keep things running successful. As a bookkeeper myself, I want to share with you the importance of having a bookkeeper right from the start, and what to look for when you're hiring one. First let's start with the why a bookkeeper? You need to know where your money is going and how much is coming in order to be successful.

I always suggest that a bookkeeping expense be part of your business plan. A bookkeeper is another main element of your business, although often left out to save money. However, not having a bookkeeper may cost money in the end. Many people think it's an avoidable expense, but it's really not, if you want to stay on top of your finances, government remittances and, in some cases, payroll.

There are a few must haves, and things you should be looking for in a bookkeeper:

A **background** in both finance and data bases. The days of pen to paper are mostly behind us, so understanding not only the accounting part but also understanding what you are doing in the program you are using is key. I have done many clean-up jobs that were the result of not understanding what the software was doing behind the scenes when the bookkeeper was working on the books.

A **good relationship** with your bookkeeper. You need to get along. I've been lucky in this area as I have a good relationship with all my clients. Being able to discuss certain issues in a friendly way that the client understands and appreciates is important. If you are not a fan of your bookkeeper it's hard to have regular conversations and keep up on your books and your finances.

Input. Your bookkeeper can only be as good as you allow them to be. If you do not keep in touch with your bookkeeper and supply them with the information and answers they require, they cannot do their job to the best of their ability for you. Having regular discussions with your bookkeeper is also important for you to understand your business, reporting and cash flow. One of the areas I look into as a bookkeeper is cost savings. If I don't have regular meetings with my clients I can't learn about their business, and that means I cannot put as in-depth a cost savings plan into place.

Communication. In this day and age it's very hard for my clients to fit time into their schedule to speak with me. The clients I am able to serve the best are the clients that make time for me. Many items can be lost via email, and I believe at a minimum you should be making time for your bookkeeper at least every quarter.

Training and certifications. Every year I continue to upgrade my skills, maintain and add new certifications. The accounting software world is ever-changing, regardless of what you are using. I have certifications in many programs, and not only do I regularly add new ones and take new courses but I also review and upgrade the ones I have. It's important to know the certifications and abilities of your bookkeeper.

Outsource or In-House

To answer this question, you need to know what it is you are looking for in a bookkeeper. What services does a bookkeeper offer and what do you require? I have clients that I offer full-service bookkeeping and I have clients that I reconcile accounts and submit tax remittances for them, and everything in between. So how do you know what services you need and what the expense will be? To know what you need, you need to know what you have. Do you have an office manager? What is it they are doing? Order entry? Payroll? Accounts payable? Accounts receivable?

These are often some of the items that cross over between an office manager and a bookkeeper. If you have knowledgeable people on staff that can do all these tasks, then most likely you require a bookkeeper just to run reports and reconcile your accounts. It's still a good idea to outsource these tasks, as this is when any mistakes made will be caught.

If you are running a very large company, you will most likely want a bookkeeper in-house on your payroll. If you are filing a weekly term of minimum forty hours a week, in-house is probably your best bet. Most small entrepreneurs do not require a full-time bookkeeper, and hiring off site allows you to save some money. You need to trust your bookkeeper in order for them to work off-site and handle your financials.

So, what is it you need your bookkeeper to do for your business? The list will vary with each business but for the most part you will find some tasks are already handled in-house and therefore outsourcing the missing piece of your financials will assist your business. Often bookkeepers offer training, so maybe you'd like to keep some tasks in-house and have some training for your staff. I offer this service both in person and through video chat.

As a bookkeeper I offer various packages to suit the needs of my clients, and I also offer personalized packages in the event I have a client looking for something that is not listed. It is imperative that you stay current with your bookkeeping. I have assisted in many clean-up jobs and these can be very difficult and confusing for both bookkeeper and client. As years go by, we often forget some things, lose paperwork, and it can often be expensive to process years at one time. At the absolute minimum, I suggest at least every quarter but monthly would be ideal to stay on top of your reporting.

Make a checklist, or join my mailing list to receive your checklist on what you require in a bookkeeper, and what you have in-house, to determine what type of bookkeeper would best suit your business requirements. Regardless of what you decide, just ensure that you keep in touch with your bookkeeper and, most importantly, that you have a bookkeeper keeping everything up to date and keeping in touch with you and your ever-changing needs to run a successful business.

Reporting

What is reporting and why do I need it? Most of us know what a profit and loss or balance sheet is, but we don't know how to use it. Often, I send out profit and loss statements, balance sheets and cash flow statements, only to find out later that they are never looked at. This is why I suggest a quarterly meeting with your bookkeeper, either live or on video chat, to review the numbers and what they mean.

You should be reviewing your numbers monthly and not just when they are requested by the bank for potential loans. Keeping on top of your reporting allows you and your bookkeeper to discuss where the high expenses are, and where the revenue is coming from. Should you be making changes in your business due to what you are seeing in your reporting?

Part of your bookkeeper's job is to send you these reports, but you also need to review them. One of the biggest challenges I have with my clients is getting them to make the time to chat with me and review their numbers. You should be looking at your numbers every month. When you file your government remittances, are you reviewing the reports or just happy knowing they have been filed? Are you reviewing your A/R and A/P on a monthly basis? Here are a few types of reports that you should be considering:

- Profit and Loss
- Balance Sheet
- Cash Flow
- Payroll / Payroll Liabilities

Why Do I Need a Bookkeeper?

A lot of this I've already answered in this chapter and yet I'm sure some of you are still staying, "I can do it myself." I've seen / heard this so many times. Here is my experience on this: You own the business, you are running the business, you are wearing many hats in your business. I have clients that own businesses and have a financial background and yet still choose to hire me. You may ask yourself why. The answer is time. It's all about time.

77

In most cases, those that choose to do it themselves fall behind because something is always on fire and requires their attention. Maybe it's a task you don't like doing so you're doing the bare minimum to keep the business going, but this will not allow you to budget and plan the way you should.

This goes back to my suggestion to put in your business plan, do what you are good at and enjoy, and hire for those tasks that you may not be as skilled at. As entrepreneurs, especially when starting out, we think we can do it all but we just can't. There is not enough time in the day. I am also guilty of this; in order to give my clients the service that they hired me for I was doing it all, I was working seven days a week around the clock and failing in some areas. Not because I am not a good bookkeeper, but because I was trying to wear every hat in my business.

In order to be successful I had to hire staff to do the jobs that I knew they were good at, and keep the work that I was exceptional at. It took a long time to realize I would be more successful hiring staff than doing it myself. Listening to my business coach, I took my own advice that I'd been telling people for years, and I hired staff to assist in my business.

I am still the final check before submitting to my clients, but I have learned that this really does work. Take my advice, don't learn the hard way, don't fall behind, hire a bookkeeper if it's not what you are great at or like to do.

In the words of my dad, "You get what you pay for." I listened to these words my entire life, and I learned he was right. I also advise this when hiring a bookkeeper. You will always find someone who is less expensive, but just make sure they are they right fit for your business and they have the knowledge that you require.

Chapter 7

Building Your Business

"Whatever good things we build end up building us."
– Jim Rohn

The Real Fun Begins

Now that you have started up your business, it is important that you know how to grow that business, and make it stand out amongst the crowd. How do you do that? Let's take a look!

Building your business is all about knowing what your customers or clients need, and what you can do that will make your business different than the ones offering the same type of work as you do. Do your research. Look around at the other companies, and what they offer clients. Look at the media and see what makes businesses stand out. Usually, if a business is doing well, you will see it referenced everywhere.

Whether you are looking online, in a newspaper, or even driving down the street; companies that have done well show their branding on practically every available instrument. They take advantage of all the different types of social media because they know that the more they highlight their company, the more business they will get.

Do your research, see what similar businesses offer their clients, and go from there. You do not need to copy what they are doing as that does not help you stand out. Instead, think of something that tops that original idea. Put yourself in your clients' shoes and think about what they might be looking for, and what would give them the motivation or desire to walk through your door instead of someone else's.

Not only do you want to give notice to your company and let possible future clients know you are there and proud to be, you want to be able to back the advertisements and show those possible clients that your company is exactly what you have raved about. Whether it is offering deals or promotions within your company, or just having a special day to support your clients; the more you do, the more they will appreciate and have other people heading your way.

As an example, you could offer a promotion for first-time clients, in order to get new people in the door. To do even more, you could offer previous clients a referral discount. The options are endless; you just need to find what works for you, and what is going to grow your business without you losing large amounts of money in the process.

Figure out what makes you and your company different from everyone else's, and run with that. People like original thoughts and ideas, so when you put something new on the table, you have a higher chance of bringing new clients in because you caught their eye with something new and refreshing. Show what makes you unique, and you will have people running through the door.

Knowing the Steps

A lot of the time, we end up knowing what we want, but are unsure of how to get there. This is where lots of planning and thinking comes into play. When you have the initial thought of creating a business, there are so many ideas racing through your head. What should I do? How should I start? What should I name my company? The questions are endless.

To figure all that out, you need to create a plan. You want a plan you can stick to, and something that is not too overwhelming, so you can avoid feeling like it is too much and eventually giving up your dream. This is what we want to avoid. Plans and goals are your best friend. They help you stay on track, and motivate you when you feel like you are taking the wrong direction in life.

When you make a big step, you are going to have some negative thoughts initially because you are doing something completely new. You are putting yourself out there, and making big moves in life. It is completely natural to feel a little overwhelmed, and question whether you are making the right choice. Let me tell you though, you are. Do not let those pesky negative thoughts get in the way of you moving mountains. You can have it all, and then some; you just need to believe in yourself and know you can make this happen.

Sit down with yourself, and get out everything onto paper (or computer if that is what you prefer). List all your goals, and what you envision your business to look like. Once you have that first step sorted out, you can start planning where you need to go next. Do you need to hire people? Do you need an office space or is it something you can do from home?

No matter how small you think the issue is, sort it out in those initial steps. Get all the what ifs figured out so you can start taking the big steps: building your business and growing it to what you first had pictured in your head. Anything you can make a plan for, do it. The more you figure out now, the less you will have to fix in the future.

Nothing to Fear With Banks and Financing

While thinking about building up your business, I am sure you have thought about the extra money that you'll need. A lot of people worry about this, and it can even deter someone from starting up a business in the first place. Financing sounds like a scary word; however, there is nothing to be afraid of, and it can be exactly what you need to create a better life for yourself. As much as borrowing money can be scary, it is worth it when it comes to growing your business and seeing your dreams become a reality.

Most businesses require some initial startup money; this is perfectly normal. There are costs for equipment, software, staff, and even costs for promoting the business such as flyers, websites, etc. While some may be able to afford those costs through savings, many people have trouble being able to afford all the extra costs that come with starting up a business, and keeping it running properly.

If you are like the majority, and cannot afford the costs on your own, you need to go through a bank or financial institution that can assist you by giving you the extra funds that are necessary to grow your business. Now all you need to do is find the right place that will loan you the money without causing you to be in over your head. Good news! There are tons of options out there that give you different interest rates, and time periods to pay off the loan.

To find the right loan or line of credit, you need to shop around. Do not make any rash decisions on a loan. This decision takes some time, as you want to make sure you are getting the best deal, and the one that fits your lifestyle. Interest rates vary depending on the bank you go to, and the type of loan you are looking at. Some give you money back, and some give lower interest rates; it all depends on what you think is best, for yourself and your business.

Ask the right questions, and if it seems too good to be true, it may very well be, but you never know unless you do the research. Once you have decided on the right bank, and the right loan, you can adjust your payments, and find the best payback option that does not leave you struggling financially.

Remember, the banks want to see you succeed as much as you do. The more you grow your business and earn money, the faster you will pay off your loan or line of credit. This will leave the banks happy too as they are getting their money back.

Avoid panic attacks when realizing you need to ask the banks for money. They are not there to trick you; they are there to help you. Listen to what they have to say, and what they are offering, and take a few days to process all the information. While you may not have the answers now, they will come to you once you see everything in front of your eyes. The loan is just a small part of your business, and it is what will help it grow and become what you envisioned.

Dealing With Your Negative Voice

Everyone has had that voice in the back of their mind telling them something bad about themselves. Whether it tells you that you are going to fail, or it tells you that you need to lose a few pounds, that voice is there for everyone! However, just because a voice is there does mean that you need to listen to it.

That voice is there to stop you. It wants to deter you from making good things happen in your life. It wants to get you to avoid taking that step. That negative voice is the scared little version of you who believes that a big step can end in failure, and that possible failure is not worth the effort to begin with. While that voice may seem to have good reasons for not putting in any effort, it is wrong, and is steering you in the wrong direction altogether.

To stop those negative thoughts, you need to first off figure out who the voice is, and where it is coming from. Is this voice your inner child? Is it a past self who has been through trauma? Figuring out why the voice is telling you these negative thoughts is key in letting all the negativity go.

As a human, you go through many ups and downs in life. Just because you have these ups and downs does not mean you will never succeed. Ups and downs are a normal part of life, so figuring out where the voice started is the first step in finding release and peace with yourself.

The next step in dealing with the negative voice is to catch those thoughts as soon as they happen. The negative thoughts tend to disappear once you take notice of them, and try to understand why they are happening. If you can pinpoint the moment you have the negative thoughts, you can usually figure out what caused them, and how to resolve them for good. If you bring that negativity to the surface, you can finally start to heal and look for a way to avoid those thoughts in the future.

A lot of the time, negative thoughts happen when you are stuck in your head, or doing something that does not involve a lot of movement. Negativity likes to show its ugly head when you are either trying to make something happen for yourself, or when you are trying to be at peace with yourself. When this happens, do something active. Go for a walk, take a swim, or go play with your kids.

The negative thoughts tend to go away when life gets in the way, so when you are stuck in your head, get back to reality, and do something that makes you feel good. Most likely, you will forget about the thoughts that popped up, and you will be back to loving who you are and the life you have.

Dealing with negative thoughts does not have to be something you battle with for a large part of your life. It can be resolved; all it takes is a little motivation and some positivity. Believe in yourself, and believe you can let go of the negativity you have been holding onto for so long. That negative energy does you no good, so let it go, feel the release as it leaves your body, and get back to the big changes you are making for yourself.

Stand Out From the Crowd

Competition is everywhere, but it is a good thing, even though it might make you sad at times. We are constantly trying to compete with other people with a similar idea or career path. You want to do your best and be the best person you can be, and despite how hard you try, sometimes seeing someone stand out from the crowd can make you feel a little defeated, but remember this. . . you have the choice to stand out from the crowd too, and be the person in the spotlight. As someone trying to grow your business, this is something that is nothing but beneficial for you, and the more you show what you are made of, the more people will take notice and want to know you and all you are a part of.

So how does one start standing out from the crowd? For me, it took some time because I did not always want to believe that what I was doing was going to be a success. We all have those doubts in the back of our mind, but at the end of the day, it's important to try and let that go so you can focus on living your best life and showing the world that you have taken this big step for a reason.

The first step in standing out from the crowd of people who are also fighting for success is to start doing your research. Do not just believe you have what it takes, really do your research and see what you have to offer that similar business don't. Take the time and see what comes off as inviting when you are looking for a certain product or type of business. Look at what others have done wrong in the past, so you can know what will work, and make your business soar!

Even better, once you have that research, take it to the next level and get creative with it. The more you can show your creative side, the more you will stand out and be the one people want to go to. This is where your digital media and webpage can come into play because you can really create something that stands out and shows possible clients all you have to offer, and how you are going to bring something new to the table.

The last and best advice I can give you to stand out from the crowd around you is to not let mistakes or any failure get in the way of making your dreams come true. Any mistake that is made is a lesson learned and a way to grow. Never let that stop you from continuing on the path you are on, and continuing to stand out. You deserve to find success, and you will make your vision a reality as long as you keep believing that you can make it possible, and finding ways to keep growing as a person and a business owner.

Something that has often been mentioned to me over the years is that I am friendly, genuine, and I listen. Truthfully, I am just me. It's much easier to show my true colours in a meeting or presentation than pretend to be someone I am not, and to my surprise this has been my biggest asset. People like me and they hire me.

Chapter 8

Time and Taxes

"Don't wait. The time will never be just right."
– Napoleon Hill

Taking Time Out

Building a business while undergoing a divorce is no easy task. It takes a lot of strength, and there will be many ups and downs along the way. The key is to never give up, and give your all. I remember in the beginning, there were days I thought it was just too much; I wanted to dig a hole and just crawl in, but I never did. I would remember my dad's words, "Buck up," and every time, I would.

Having a support system has definitely helped, I didn't always have much of a support system. But the few people I had were what got me through the hard days. My biggest support system always has been, and still is, my kids. My daughter would say to me, "Mom, you can do anything. You wanted a house so you worked hard and you got one. =You've done it all, Mom."

My son was always there to give me a hug when I needed it, especially when the days were tough. The smile of my two kids were what kept me going every single day.

I had to remind myself to take time out, spend time with the kids and with friends. There is always something to be done when you own a business, but taking time out makes you better at what you are doing. It was probably the hardest task for me, as I don't want to let down my clients, and I don't want to miss deadlines. I always told myself, "Just a few more hours."

Sadly though, a few more hours often turns into many, and then days go by. When you get so wrapped up in the business side of your life, you forget to take time out to do things that benefit you and make you feel good about the life you are living. You may work endless hours and earn a large income which benefits your life; however, it does not do you any good when you are neglecting other parts of yourself that need care too. To create time for myself, and time to spend with others, I started putting my "time out" in my calendar.

I started scheduling that time to have fun and actually enjoy life. Spending all your time and energy on your work may seem like a good option to get you to that next stage in your life, but it is not going to help you in the long term. It will affect your health, your emotions, and really get you feeling down because you are not taking that time to enjoy life. A bonfire on a Friday night with the kids is the best time out there that I know.

No matter how capable you think you are, it is important and necessary to take that time away from your busy work life. Hang out with the kids, have that dinner date with your friend that you have been postponing. You deserve to have it all, and you can. Take the time to care about yourself and see what good can come from it.

Training and Education

For most people, schooling usually ends when they graduate from either college or university with a program that will give them a career that will stick with them. This is not always the case for everyone though, and many people end up realizing they want to continue with their education and training. There could be many reasons for this. Maybe they decided the original program they took was not quite right for them. Maybe they got into the career, and realized it was not a good fit.

Whatever the reason is, continuing your education is nothing but beneficial. When you continue with training and education, you gain more knowledge, you gain confidence, and you give yourself the right building blocks to create an amazing future for yourself. There is no ending point for how much knowledge you can absorb. Your options are endless when you give yourself the opportunity to further your education.

Sadly, now we are in a world where competition surrounds us. There are people fighting for your job constantly, and trying to prove that they can do it better than you. Why let them win when you can keep growing and learning and make it so nothing can stop you from achieving greatness? Do not let anyone get in the way of making your dreams come true. You are only as powerful as you think you are. If you keep telling yourself "This is as far as I can get". . . then that is truly as far as you are going to get.

Instead, do not create a limit for yourself. Keep pushing, keep learning, and keep believing you have what it takes. Whether it is going back to school, taking up some new training, or even going to a weekend retreat to learn a new skill. . . it is going to benefit you to further your education and your training, in so many ways.

Taxes

We all pay them, and we all dislike them, but there is no escaping government taxes. My experience as a bookkeeper is the clients that struggle the most are those that have fallen behind with taxes. It's important to figure out what taxes apply to your business and at the same time, what government grants apply to your business.

Keeping on top of your taxes is a sure way to keep a lot of the stress out of your business. Be sure to research or talk to a qualified representative to find out what taxes apply in your situation. I find that people just don't do their research, and are unaware of what is available to them and their business. There are ways to use tax credits that will assist you at the end of the year so that it is a pain-free process, and actually can benefit you too.

I also always file my clients' various tax remittances on a regular basis, and in order to do that, you must have your bookkeeping up to date. Falling behind in your bookkeeping most likely means you will also fall behind with your tax remittances and pay high interest fees due to this. You also risk the chance of having your cash flow stopped, depending on the severity of what taxes and how far you have fallen behind.

When you keep track of your bookkeeping, you know the exact amounts you spend, as well as the money that is coming in. The more you can keep track of, the better it will be for you when tax season comes by again. You can actually use a lot of your expenses (if they are used for your business) as another tax break to make it so you either owe nothing, or very little at the end of the year; and sometimes, you may even end up with a return. It is all about what you know, and how it can help you in the long run.

If you are unaware of some of the tax breaks available to you, do your research, or speak to a professional who can help you understand the many ways that your taxes can be an easy process, without having you rip out your hair from high stress.

Awards

Awards are a great way to promote your business; do a little bit of research and find out what is available to your business. Possibilities include local awards from your community, awards for your business classification, and awards for you personally. Put yourself and your business out there for the best opportunity for your business to grow. The more you can get people looking, the better.

Your business is only as good as you make it. The more work you put into getting noticed, the more it is going to pay off. If you choose to stay on the sidelines and avoid getting your business properly marketed, then you will most likely stay in the same position you have been for some time now. Changes only happen when you put in the effort to make those changes. If you want to get noticed, then take the opportunity to use every marketing tool available to you.

You don't have to win every award you are nominated for; just being nominated for an award is a great achievement for your business. A nomination also gets your foot in the door to possible new customers. While you may not have won the award, you stood out enough to be one of the businesses to get nominated, and that in itself is usually plenty to get you noticed. Don't go unnoticed anymore. . . find out what sets you apart and market that.

Business Plan

When trying to create a business plan, it can sometimes be a tad confusing to know what exactly to include. Maybe you do not want to add unnecessary information, or maybe you are just a perfectionist and do not want to take a wrong step in creating your plan. Well, you no longer have to worry! I will walk you step by step through what is usually included in a business plan, and how to get started.

Let's start by looking at what a business plan is. Simply put, a business plan includes all the plans you have for your business. It involves adding in the steps you have to take, why you are choosing to grow this business, and what your goals are when creating the business. It is a layout of what you plan to do, and what you would like to see happen within your business.

Your business plan is there to guide you, and keep you on track with the goals you have set in place for yourself, and your business. Many new business owners struggle to stay on track because this is completely new to them. If you are just starting out in your own business, or even starting out new in a company in general, it can be extremely beneficial to you to make a business plan to help you stay focused and know the next step you should be taking.

You may be the most organized person in the world, and I can still guarantee that having a business plan set in place is going to help you dramatically. You are going to know each and every day what you are doing, and why you are doing it. You will start to see everything fall into place when you have this business plan, and it will help you to avoid any not so good surprises that might threaten to come your way. When you have a good business plan, nothing is going to be able to stop you.

Below are some of the many benefits that go along with creating a business plan:

- You avoid making the big mistakes that can happen when growing a business. Many businesses can reach the five-year mark; however, it is difficult when you do not create short- and long-term goals for yourself.

- A business plan can help you to work around the mistakes that people usually make when growing a business, because you will have steps set in place that avoid them. Plan ahead as much as you can to avoid making big mistakes that are difficult to overcome.

- It helps you to make tough decisions. When you have a business plan, you can help yourself through the hard decisions you have to make because you have a reference to look back on to see the original plans you had set in place for your business. Business decisions can be really overwhelming; however, when you have something to look back on, those decisions become a lot clearer to you, and you end up knowing the next step to take.

- You are creating a guide for other future employees. While you may not be thinking about hiring anyone to assist you quite yet, it might be something you want to do in the future. When you have a business plan created, it can serve as a guide for future employees to look over to better understand your work objectives and the goals you have for your business.

Chapter 9

Celebrating Success

"Success is not final, failure is not fatal:
it is the courage to continue that counts."
– Winston Churchill

Success at its Finest

That wonderful feeling of success is a great feeling no matter who you are; however, many people lose the idea of success because once they achieve one goal, they move right on to the next one without celebrating that they accomplished the original goal. It is always about the next thing, instead of focusing on what they did well and applauding themselves for that.

Success should be celebrated, no matter how big or small the success is. You need to give yourself the acknowledgement that you did a great job, whether or not you achieved the goal in the time frame you intended, or you didn't stick to the exact plan you had set in place. Life is all about being proud of the amazing things you did so you can feel the motivation to achieve the next goal you have created for yourself.

It is important to remember, though, that celebrating and rewarding are too very different things. Celebrating is when give yourself praise for the process you took and the result it gave. Rewarding is similar but instead of giving yourself a pat on the back, you reward yourself with something tangible.

While it is great to reward yourself, you should keep that for specific situations or goals, rather than for every goal you achieve.

Success can be celebrated in many ways; it just depends on who you are and what makes you feel good. Celebrating your success in a healthy way can start with reflecting on what you did, and the steps you took to get there. You can ask yourself questions like:

- How did I get to this place?
- What did I do to make it happen?
- What strengths did I use?
- How did all of this benefit me?

Asking yourself simple questions like those above can help you to understand both what you did and how well you did. It can get you to appreciate the steps you took, and the work and effort that was put into it. Make yourself feel good about all you have done, instead of just moving on to the next goal. Savour it. Let everything process in your head so you can truly be celebratory.

Celebrating your success with people you are close to is also a great way to internalize the fact that you did a great job. The more people you have to support you, the better you feel. Let others know the work you put in and how it paid off. Share your experiences with others and join in on the celebration together. You worked incredibly hard to reach your goal, so it is important to let the people you care about know this so you can feel that much better knowing that other people see the effort you made.

There are many ways to celebrate success. Give it a try and see how good you feel afterwards. Tell yourself how well you did, and receive compliments when others let you know too. Success deserves to be celebrated no matter what!

Overcoming the Voice Inside Your Head

Overcoming that little voice in your head can be quite tricky, especially when you have been listening to it for as long as you can remember. The voices inside your head include any negative thoughts you think or feel about yourself. They are what deter you from making big decisions in your life because "You can't do this" or "You are going to fail."

That voice rears its ugly head when you are trying to get a great job, when you are trying to build a business, and during any other important activity or event in your life. It is there to stop you from taking the next step because you have told yourself before that you can't do it, or you are afraid that you will fail.

Fear is a normal part of the process when becoming an entrepreneur. Of course you are going to have fear when making a huge decision, but that does not mean you are making the wrong decision. Fear and the voice in your head go hand in hand. Its goal is to stop you so you do not have to feel overwhelmed and scared any longer.

To drown out the voice inside your head, you need to first start by understanding where it's coming from and why it is showing up at that specific moment. Once you can narrow it down to one specific concern, you can start to work it out in your head, and see why you are anxious. You can ask yourself important questions to get to the root issue. Then, you can start to heal, and focus on the goals you have set for yourself.

It's important to remember not to fight the voice though. As much as you want to yell at it and tell it to go away, that is not going to resolve the issue and make the voice go away. It gains energy on you fueling back at it, so instead, say thank you, and calmly sort out what is happening and why you feel that way. The sooner you get those answers, the faster that voice will mellow out, and the better off you will be.

Let that voice know the opposite of what it is telling you. For an example, if your voice is telling you that you are not good enough, say right back to it that you are good enough and you can make anything happen for yourself. The more positive thoughts you tell yourself, the more that negative voice will fade. You just need to replace the negative with the positive.

Lastly, the voices you hear usually come around when you are feeling a lack of comfort with something, or someone. When you start hearing those little thoughts, let yourself know that you are comfortable with feeling uncomfortable. Tell yourself that everything will be okay, and you are doing what you are meant to do. The more you can tell yourself that you are okay with what is happening around you, and how you are feeling, the less those thoughts will show up, and the better you will ultimately feel.

Do not let those thoughts get in the way of making big changes in your life. If it is something you are passionate about, then try to let those worries fade away so you can focus on your goals.

The Naysayers

The naysayers are quite similar to the negative voice in your head, except for the fact that they are people around you, and usually close to you, telling you to stop what you are doing because they don't believe you can succeed. This is sometimes worse than the voice inside your head, as it is people around you telling you to give up when they should be building you up.

Just like with the voices in your head, you need to remember not to let it get to you. Not everyone is going to have a positive opinion, and that is something that you need to accept. As much as there will be people rooting you on and telling you to keep going, there will be people telling you the exact opposite, and it is up to you to decide which people to listen to.

Listening to the negative thoughts of others will only stop you from continuing, and will make you feel like you made a mistake to begin with. Instead, drown it out. If someone has something negative to say about the big steps you are making in your life, then maybe you need to question if they are a healthy and positive person to be in your life.

If you hear a negative thought from someone around you, replace it with a positive one. Tell yourself you are doing this for you, and the path you are on is the one you should be on. You and only you can decide what is best for you and your future, so if someone is trying their best to stop you from taking those next steps, then ignore it, and focus on you, and the amazing steps you are making in your life.

Level Up

We are all born into this world a blank slate. We all start out the same way, just learning how to navigate through this crazy thing we call life. As we go through the years, we learn that, eventually, we want more in our lives, and want to "level up" and be that next best version of ourselves.

This section is all about learning how to grow and master challenging yourself as well as bettering yourself each day. Let's start by talking about goals. We all know how amazing creating goals is, and how they can help guide us through any challenge we come across, or any new path we want to take in life. Sometimes though, when we focus on all those little things, it takes away from the big picture and the WHY in starting your business and putting all this effort in.

When you go back to looking at the big picture. . . that big goal, you start to feel motivated again and want to keep levelling up. You can only feel that need to level up when you are content and happy with where you are, and it all starts with the big steps you are making in your life. Stop stressing out about all those little steps. . . they will come. Instead, focus on it as a whole and you feel start to feel proud and want to keep doing more.

Levelling up in life becomes automatic when you start seeking out more of those wonderful feel good moments. You know those moments I am talking about. It's those moments that make you feel energetic and proud about the journey you are on. Those moments are what you should be striving for every day so you can keep getting your motivation to level up so you can be the best you that you can be!

If you want to level up, start showing yourself and the world what you are made of, and that you are unstoppable. When you do that, the rest will fall into place, and you will have a strength that cannot be taken away from you.

Share Your Success

With any success, big or small, you should take the time to share it with the people who care about you and want to see you achieve your dreams. Sharing your success not only makes you feel good initially, it also keeps motivates you to want to achieve that next goal, or succeed at the next step on your big plan.

So often, we are told not to "brag" or show others something they themselves do not have. When it comes to your success though, you should not avoid telling the people who matter in your life the amazing changes you are making, no matter where they are in their own life.

Trust me, no matter what stage they are in, they are going to be proud of you, and love the fact that you are succeeding in your life. If they truly care about you and the life you are living, you should be excited to share those moments with them, and let them know how unstoppable you are.

Sharing your successes with others around you may also motivate them to do more with their own lives. If they see you doing great things, they will want to join in and see what happens when they take that step and strive for more themselves. And just like that, you will have a circle of people supporting one another and giving each other the motivation to be successful.

Defining What Success is to You

Success looks different to everyone. The definition of success is created by you, and in your own mind, so you can really determine what success looks like to you, and it does not mean becoming a millionaire. Success is whatever you deem to be successful. . . not what anyone else believes.

It also doesn't make it any easier when everywhere around you, ads, commercials, and celebrities are trying to make a clear definition on what success is, and while these forms of marketing may show successful people, there are many forms of it, and it's important for you to know that it does not always look like a large bank account, and everything you could ask for.

Here are some definitions of success that can help you to feel motivated and see that you are definitely on the right path:

- Success is believing in yourself, and believing you can make anything possible.
- Success is taking care of your needs both mentally, physically, professionally, and emotionally.
- Success is learning that "no" is perfectly fine to say, and at times needed.
- Success is overcoming the fears that have been holding you back.
- Success is never giving up despite what tries to get you down.
- Success is making sure you celebrate even the smallest of victories.
- Success is learning to stand up for yourself and what you believe in.
- Success is remembering to keep finding that passion for life.
- Success is setting goals and not giving up.
- Success is always doing your best, and knowing what you are capable of!

Chapter 10

A Final Word

"Start where you are. Use what you have.
Do what you can."
– Arthur Ashe

Keeping Up the Momentum

Remember you are the heart and soul of the business, and when you stop the business stops. The business needs you to thrive, not just a piece of you but all of you. So how do you keep going when you feel like you have the weight of the world on your shoulders? You keep going because this is what you love to do. Divorce is tough; use those emotions and pour them into your business.

My entire life I've always said, "My glass is half full, NOT half empty." And I use that in my business too. If things are not going the way they should be, I don't stop and cry, I push through it and work harder to get the job done and keep my clients excited and grateful along the way. I used to stop and cry, but that didn't pay the bills, that didn't do me any good, and nothing got done. There were days I didn't want to get out of bed, but I forced myself, and once I dove into my work and saw the results I was capable of, the ugly stuff drifted away and the sun shone bright.

Choose your clients, don't let them choose you. Sometimes when we are scared we accept anything, because believe that something is better than nothing. Not true; and I learned this the hard way.

If you have a client that is consuming your time with no return or little return, move on, nicely. You will get to know your ideal clients, just as I did. I now turn people away. It's not that I don't want to help them; I'd help everyone for free if I could. It's because I need to grow and scale my business to be successful, and I can't if I am not making any money all week.

I now have a list of criteria that I go through, and if potential clients don't meet the criteria, I kindly refer them to someone else.

Now this is not true of all industries; I would not advise that you turn away someone in line to order food at a restaurant, but I am sure there are times when you have to politely ask people to leave. My point here is use your common sense, choose the people that you can work with, and that want to work with you.

Keeping your momentum going is like navigating a triangle that has emotions on one side, financial on one side, and physical on the other. And we just keep bouncing from side to side of that triangle until we find the right balance and we smoothly glide around it with a bounce in our step, and a smile on our face. MOMENTUM – Movement on Money, Escape Negative Tasks, Understand Miracles.

Pivoting With World Changes

In 2020, the world changed, and although I'd been through many changes in my lifetime I had not been through life-altering world changes as an adult and entrepreneur. My dad would tell me stories of the depression and the struggles they had. I was living through the technology change and for me this was only moving my business forward. I was changing with the times to benefit me and my clients.

Then 2020 happened, and it affected most businesses in one way or another. Some struggled more than others but we were all affected. For some of us it was a wake-up call that we need to change with the times and not get complacent in our business. I was one of the lucky ones as I continued to work, although big changes happened along the way.

As a woman, entrepreneur, and small business owner, I did not qualify for many benefits or subsidies being offered both in business and personally. Some of my clients were struggling to keep open and pay their bills, and this meant that I was struggling with cash flow.

Once again I had to think outside the box as to how I could continue to grow and be successful through such tough times. It's that out of the box thinking that will continue to grow your business and allow you to be successful.

We all got hit one way or another on this, maybe personally, maybe professionally, but when you are self-employed, personal and professional issues often run together. Along with some of the changes from 2020 I was also dealing with some big personal changes that almost closed down my business. The loss of both my dad and my brother paralyzed me and my business.

Although I was going through the motions and keeping up, I was struggling, and it showed. At the same time it was a great lesson in life. My dad was my mentor, my support, and the one who would guide me to the light through the trees. After losing him I thought I couldn't do it anymore. A year later I lost my brother, and that made getting out of bed in the morning even harder. Then one day, sitting in my backyard listening to the cardinals sing and thinking of them both, I realized it was up to me to move forward and be successful and stop feeling so sad. I also knew that it was what they would want me to do. Yes, the giggles from my brother and the support from my dad always helped me along the way, but I had to make a choice to pick myself up and be successful, or fail if I continued to stay on the path I was on. I made the choice to be successful.

Cash Flow in Your Business

Cash flow is so important, and something business owners often overlook. I bet you look at your balance sheet and profit and loss, but when was the last time you looked at a cash flow report? I look at my cash flow on a regular basis. Being a service business and a startup, out of necessity I've learned a lot along the way and I am trying to share with you on a more personal level and not high level.

I had to make many changes to keep the cash flow in my business. I went through a phase where I was always stealing from Peter to pay Paul. It was stressful. The big one for me was slow paying clients; how could I fix this? New clients were brought in on retainer, I did up the proposal and no work was started until I received the money.

I had a hard time not working for those clients that I knew would pay me but hadn't yet. I moved to monthly billing, and this assisted my clients to know that every month they had a bill to be paid. Some even chose to be put on reoccurring so that their credit card was charged monthly and they didn't have to worry about it.

These small changes made a big difference in my business. If you are watching your cash flow and accounts receivable, you can stay on top of this before you get yourself into trouble, like I once did. Going to pay bills and having the money in the bank is a lot less stressful than looking at your A/R and having to spend a day, of lost income, trying to get clients to pay their bills.

I also realized that I couldn't be so nice in order to be successful. Instead of calling or emailing and saying, "I really would appreciate it if you paid me today as your invoice is very overdue," I starting being more firm with my clients. I found if I gave an inch, some would take a mile. I needed to find a balance between understanding of hard times and not sacrificing my own business in doing so.

Hiring Staff and the Challenges

Hiring staff has always been a challenge for me. Giving up control; will they be as good as I am? If I do the work that is more money in my pocket. But the truth is it gets very overwhelming, and working 7 days a week 14 hours a day catches up with you. The first challenge in hiring is letting go. If you've always done it yourself, this is probably the most difficult task.

I started with part-time people and hired students that were interested in accounting. If the proper training is in place this can be very successful. Watching a student get excited about your industry and thinking this could be a career path for them is very rewarding. The mentee all of a sudden becomes the mentor and you see why people give their time to mentor others.

Setting the pay grade is also a tough one, as you want people to be interested in the job so they produce good work, but part of their interest involves their income. If it's all about the money I truly don't want those people; I want people that are excited about the job too. You need to find a balance between what your staff is worth and what you can afford. Will you be hiring sub-contract, part-time or full-time? What taxes will you be paying in order to do so? This all needs to go into your budget.

The interview process is something most of us dread. Even with a small business I highly suggest going through the process, calling references and making sure you find a good fit. Know what credentials you're looking for. Are you willing to train or do you want someone with experience?

Finding the perfect fit every time doesn't always work out. Be willing to work with your employees; don't forget about them. I always make sure there is a personal element as well. How do they like the atmosphere? Is there something I can do to help them succeed? And even just a "How is your day going? And how are you?" For the most part the success of your employee is a result of you.

Dreams vs Reality

It took me a while to get out of my head with my dreams and face the reality of my life and my business. I had dreams of grandeur, but the reality was I had to walk before I ran. When you are one hundred percent dependent on yourself, building a clientele to ensure the income is there to pay the bills and put food on the table is number one. I personally did not take huge risks in the beginning. I wanted a house for me and my kids, and I had to build the business one step at a time to get there.

Isn't that what we all want? Some sense of stability and peace? We all want to feel like everything is going to be okay, and that is all a part of discovering what are dreams are versus what we can make a reality. We all want that perfect life, just sometimes, it takes a little longer to find the path you were meant to be on, but once you are on it, you are going to feel this shift in your life, and you'll know that you are exactly where you are supposed to be.

Writing everything down definitely assisted with the process for me. What did I need right now and how many clients would it take to get there? The drive I had to succeed allowed for my dreams and reality to often cross paths. The motivation that was inside kept me going even on the days when I felt like nothing was going quite right.

For example, I didn't think I'd be buying a house for the first five years, but I did it in three. I still have big dreams for my future and my business, but I do keep things in check. The problem for me with the big dreams is I wasn't focusing on today, I was focusing on tomorrow. In order to be successful, I had to focus on today first. As much as you want to focus on the future, and that is what goals are all about, you still need to focus on the present and what is happening right now around you.

Keep those dreams in your mind, and keep striving to make them a reality each and every day, because you and I both know, you will get there. Just remember to have a balance, and learn to stay in both the present and future so you can focus on what you need to do right now, but also have those future goals set in your mind so that you have a pathway to success!

And in Conclusion

I am pleased you have followed me on my journey, and I hope some of my experiences have helped you along the way. This is not a how-to on building a business, but more of a story about my personal wins and losses along the way.

I was told on a regular basis, "Just get a REAL job." I was pushed down more than I was raised up, but I never stopped. I kept working hard for the success of my business and didn't listen to the naysayers that would have turned my direction. My goal with this book is to let you know you can do it. Going through divorce is hard, raising kids on your own is hard, starting and running a business is hard! Put them all together and it's even harder. My goal with this book is to let you know you are not alone. Stay in touch through my website, email, and social media sites. Share your story on my Facebook page.

Let the kids help you. No matter what the age, with the exception of babies. Big or small, you will find they want to help Mommy because she's doing it all alone. The praise I get from my kids is heartwarming. My kids step up and help without me even asking now; it's just part of the routine so Mommy can work to pay the bills. Now both of my kids work in my business to help me get some free time to spend with them. When they help me I reward them with my time. For my daughter it's walking the dog or a day at the barn. My son enjoys movie and popcorn or a night playing games. Bonfires with marshmallows is a special treat for all of us.

The biggest lesson I learned along the way is that anger and hurt hold me back from succeeding. I was able to compartmentalize a lot of the issues I was having to move forward with a smile. I stopped dealing with everything, every minute of every day, and started dealing with the things in front of me. I stopped trying to control the things I couldn't control, and this allowed me to be happy every single day. I allowed myself to be sad when I needed to be, but not for long periods of time.

Most importantly, take time for you. I don't get a lot of time to spend with friends and family, but I do take time to go to the farm where my daughter keeps her horse. Most of this book was written sitting in the back of my car at the farm. It is peaceful and surrounded by nature; what more could I ask for?

For some, maybe it's a day at the spa, or a BBQ with friends and family. For me, it's a peaceful day at the farm with my daughter. Sometimes my son joins us, and barn friends that always make me smile and laugh. Taking a break even through the busiest of times can mean the difference in your wellbeing and success.

The best thing I did for me was get my dog! He keeps me company when the kids are gone and I am working. He tells me when I've been working too long and it's time for a break or playtime. Be sure to accept the support from wherever you get it along the way. It will come in places you didn't expect at times. In the beginning, I was too proud to say I needed help, and then I learned that people wanted to help me because they liked me and I had been there for them. It never hurts to ask for help!

And remember . . . You Got This!!!

About the Author

Kim Edmiston has been an established bookkeeper for over 20 years. She started her career in 1995, establishing the accounting division for a computer technical support corporation. She continued her career in the financial industry working for Davis + Henderson in database management -- financial division, as a billing analyst.

Kim moved to a small 10 acre farm in 2005 with her husband at the time and two horses, Elvis and Pricilla, and their dogs, Ben and Elijah. In 2006 their daughter Alex was born and in 2008 they welcomed their son Brayden.

Over the next few years Kim worked as an entrepreneur with a digital media company, alongside her own bookkeeping business. Kim's parents showed her the importance of family, and she spent many years working in the community to support moms, children, and families through fun events. She served on a community collaborative board to build on the strengths of children and youth in the community, and also pitched, produced and co-hosted a TV show on local Rogers TV programming to further assist families in the community.

In 2015 Kim and her husband separated, and she started a new path as a single mom. She rebranded her bookkeeping business under the name of AB Plus K Virtual Bookkeeping Services, and worked hard to be able to be home for her children while earning an income to provide for them.

During this time Kim felt very alone and wanted to do something to empower other women to achieve their goals. However, the thought of her journey to achieve success written in book form was a dream she didn't think would come true ... until now.

www.ingramcontent.com/pod-product-compliance
Lightning Source LLC
Chambersburg PA
CBHW072156090426

42740CB00012B/2294